Discussions of George Eliot

DISCUSSIONS OF LITERATURE

General Editor JOSEPH H. SUMMERS, Washington University

Edited by

Hamlet	J. C. LEVENSON, University of Minnesota
Alexander Pope	RUFUS A. BLANSHARD, University of Connecticut
The Novel	ROGER SALE, Amherst College
George Eliot	RICHARD STANG, Carleton College
Moby-Dick	MILTON R. STERN, University of Connecticut

DISCUSSIONS

OF

GEORGE ELIOT

Edited with an Introduction by

Richard Stang

CARLETON COLLEGE

D. C. Heath and Company

BOSTON

Copyright © 1960 by D. C. Heath and Company

No part of the material covered by this copyright may be reproduced
in any form without written permission of the publisher.

Printed in the United States of America (6 B 0)

CONTENTS

History of Criticism of G. Eliot

HENRY JAMES, The Novels of George Eliot	3
HENRY JAMES, The Life of George Eliot	8
HENRY JAMES, *Daniel Deronda:* A Conversation	13
LESLIE STEPHEN, George Eliot	17
MARCEL PROUST, Notes on George Eliot	25
VIRGINIA WOOLF, George Eliot	26
LORD DAVID CECIL, George Eliot	31
S. L. BETHELL, The Novels of George Eliot	39
F. R. LEAVIS, George Eliot	46
V. S. PRITCHETT, George Eliot	56
JOAN BENNETT, Vision and Design	62
BASIL WILLEY, George Eliot	68
BARBARA HARDY, Imagery in George Eliot's Last Novels	77
QUENTIN ANDERSON, George Eliot in *Middlemarch*	85
JEROME THALE, George Eliot's Fable for Her Times: *Silas Marner*	95
JEROME THALE, The Darkened World: *Daniel Deronda*	100

INTRODUCTION

Just a hundred years ago (1859), in what was probably the earliest general estimate of the novels of George Eliot (only *Adam Bede* and *The Mill on the Floss* had then appeared), R. H. Hutton, an influential editor and critic, announced the coming of age of English fiction. For the first time a novelist had appeared who could pierce below the "social surface" and "give us more insight into the deeper roots of character." Thirteen years later, in a review of *Middlemarch*, Henry James praised the solidity of George Eliot's created world and the density of the "atmosphere of interests and passions and loves and enmities and strivings," and went on to notice the "constant presence of thought, of generalizing instinct, of *brain*, in a word, behind her observation [which] gives the latter its great value and her whole manner its high superiority." Though a great admirer of *Middlemarch*, James was disturbed by the all-inclusiveness of George Eliot's study of provincial life: "Its diffuseness . . . makes it too copious a dose of pure fiction. If we write novels so, how shall we write History?" Hence her book, in spite of its undoubted greatness, lacked form; it was not "an organized, molded, balanced composition, gratifying the reader with a sense of design and construction. . . ."

After George Eliot's death in 1881, which was the occasion for almost extravagant eulogy, her reputation among many of the younger writers began to decline rapidly, though to judge by the number of sets of her complete works published between 1885 and 1920, the general public continued to read her as devotedly as it ever had in the 1860's and 1870's.

In one of his earliest surviving letters, William Butler Yeats announced confidently in the late eighties that after going through four of George Eliot's books he would not read a fifth: her world lacked beauty. "Tito, her most famous character, is as interesting as a cat on the vivisection table. In him there is none of that beauty that Hugo gave to everything he touched, not only to Esmeralda but to the hunchback. In literature nothing that is not beautiful has any right to exist." In addition "she is too reasonable. I hate reasonable people, the activity of their brains sucks all of the blood out of their hearts." Equally unsympathetic, George Moore was certain that her virtues "were not enough to save her from the whirling, bubbling flood of time; her books have gone down like the mill [on the Floss]. Light things have floated; hers have sunk out of sight." Her disappearance was certainly confirmed in 1936 when any consideration of her novels was pointedly omitted from *The English Novelists*, edited by Derek Verschoyle, a volume that was intended "to trace the *development* of English fiction . . . by discussing the writers who have made the most important contributions to its growth—to provide, as it were, a critical genealogy of the best fiction that is being written in the English language today." One can detect in the essays by Bethell, Mrs. Woolf, Pritchett, and Cecil which appear in the present volume—all written between 1920 and 1946—a strongly apologetic note for dealing with a writer so obviously "dated." Even as late as 1948 an eminent scholar wrote, "No other Victorian novelist of major rank is so little

viii   Introduction

read today" because her stories were but
"vehicles" for her ideas. Today, as a reading of almost any recent discussion of the
English novel will make clear, even if one
does not particularly like the novels of
George Eliot he cannot dismiss them as
negligible. It is now generally agreed
among literary critics and historians that
1859, which saw the publication of *Adam
Bede,* was one of the most significant years
for the development of the English novel
and that George Eliot's place as one of the
major literary figures of the nineteenth
century seems secure. Dr. Leavis's praise
of her novels no longer sounds excessive,
nor does the great labor and erudition ex-
pended on Professor Haight's seven-volume
edition of *The George Eliot Letters* seem
out of proportion to the intrinsic importance of the novels that George Eliot has
left us. Fifteen years ago the inclusion of
George Eliot in such a series as the present
might have seemed questionable; twenty-
five years ago it would have been impossible; today it is almost inevitable.

The selections in this volume should give
the reader a rather complete history of the
critical reputation of George Eliot's novels,
beginning with Henry James's review in the
Atlantic Monthly in 1866 of the first collected edition (before the appearance of
Middlemarch and *Daniel Deronda*), and
ending with Jerome Thale's *The Novels of
George Eliot,* 1959. The essays included
here run from the very delicate impres-
sionistic criticism of Proust and Virginia
Woolf to the close analytic reading of F. R.
Leavis. I have tried to include the most interesting treatments of as many significant
aspects of her work as possible: Joan Bennett on the form of the typical George Eliot

novel, S. L. Bethell on the development of
her prose style, Barbara Hardy on the imagery of the late novels, Basil Willey on
the relation of the thought—especially the
theory of art and the religion—of George
Eliot to that of the other important Victorian writers. There are also extended discussions of *Silas Marner* and *Daniel Deronda* by Jerome Thale, of *Romola* and
Felix Holt by F. R. Leavis, of *Middlemarch*
by Quentin Anderson, and of *Daniel Deronda* by Henry James. Though the emphasis—as is natural today—is on the
late novels, *Adam Bede* and *The Mill on
the Floss* are discussed by V. S. Pritchett,
Joan Bennett, Henry James, and Lord
David Cecil.

A reading of the thirteen critics presented here should leave the student somewhat
uncomfortable with many of the critical
assumptions about the art of fiction in fashion today. For George Eliot does interrupt
her story to make direct and often didactic
comments to the reader, she stops the action
at dramatic moments in the story to analyze
the psychological states of her characters,
and she creates such a host of minor characters and incidents that the typical George
Eliot novel might seem almost formless
today. As to the major critical question
raised by the novels of George Eliot—why
the marked difference in quality between
novels like *Romola* and *Middlemarch* and
within novels like *Felix Holt* and *Daniel
Deronda?*—the student should see from the
varied attempts at answers by Henry James,
Leslie Stephen, Virginia Woolf, and F. R.
Leavis that the effort to resolve such a
problem brings us to the fundamental question of what we are looking for in great
fiction.

RICHARD STANG

Discussions of George Eliot

DISCUSSIONS OF LITERATURE

George Eliot

Henry James

The Novels of George Eliot

. . . Her opportunities for the study of the manners of the solid lower classes have evidently been very great. We have her word for it that she has lived much among the farmers, mechanics, and small traders of that central region of England which she has made known to us under the name of Loamshire. The conditions of the popular life in this district in that already distant period to which she refers the action of most of her stories—the end of the last century and the beginning of the present— were so different from any that have been seen in America, that an American, in treating of her books, must be satisfied not to touch upon the question of their accuracy and fidelity as pictures of manners and customs. He can only say that they bear strong internal evidence of truthfulness.

If he is a great admirer of George Eliot, he will indeed be tempted to affirm that they *must* be true. They offer a completeness, a rich density of detail, which could be the fruit only of a long term of conscious contact,—such as would make it much more difficult for the author to fall into the perversion and suppression of facts, than to set them down literally. It is very probable that her colours are a little too bright, and her shadows of too mild a gray, that the sky of her landscapes is too

sunny, and their atmosphere too redolent of peace and abundance. Local affection may be accountable for half of this excess of brilliancy; the author's native optimism is accountable for the other half.

I do not remember, in all her novels, an instance of gross misery of any kind not directly caused by the folly of the sufferer. There are no pictures of vice or poverty or squalor. There are no rags, no gin, no brutal passions. That average humanity which she favours is very *borné* in intellect, but very genial in heart, as a glance at its representatives in her pages will convince us. . . .

To a certain extent, I think *Silas Marner* holds a higher place than any of the author's works. It is more nearly a masterpiece; it has more of that simple, rounded, consummate aspect, that absence of loose ends and gaping issues, which marks a classical work. What was attempted in it, indeed, was within more immediate reach than the heart-trials of Adam Bede and Maggie Tulliver. A poor, dull-witted, disappointed Methodist cloth-weaver; a little golden-haired foundling child; a well-meaning, irresolute country squire, and his patient, childless wife;—these, with a chorus of simple, beer-loving villagers, make up the *dramatis personae*. More than

First printed in the *Atlantic Monthly* in 1866; reprinted in *Views and Reviews*, ed. LeRoy Phillips, Boston, Ball Publishing Company, 1908.

any of its brother-works, *Silas Marner*, I think, leaves upon the mind a deep impression of the grossly material life of agricultural England in the last days of the old *régime*,—the days of full-orbed Toryism, of Trafalgar and of Waterloo, when the invasive spirit of French domination threw England back upon a sense of her own insular solidity, and made her for the time doubly, brutally, morbidly English. Perhaps the best pages in the work are the first thirty, telling the story of poor Marner's disappointments in friendship and in love, his unmerited disgrace, and his long, lonely twilight-life at Raveloe, with the sole companionship of his loom, in which his muscles moved "with such even repetition, that their pause seemed almost as much a constraint as the holding of his breath."

Here, as in all George Eliot's books, there is a middle life and a low life; and here, as usual, I prefer the low life. In *Silas Marner*, in my opinion, she has come nearest the mildly rich tints of brown and gray, the mellow lights and the undreadful corner-shadows of the Dutch masters whom she emulates. . . .

In all those of our author's books which have borne the name of the hero or heroine,—*Adam Bede, Silas Marner, Romola,* and *Felix Holt,*—the person so put forward has really played a subordinate part. The author may have set out with the intention of maintaining him supreme; but her material has become rebellious in her hands, and the technical hero has been eclipsed by the real one. Tito is the leading figure in *Romola*. The story deals predominantly, not with Romola as affected by Tito's faults, but with Tito's faults as affecting first himself, and incidentally his wife. Godfrey Cass, with his lifelong secret, is by right the hero of *Silas Marner*. Felix Holt, in the work which bears his name, is little more than an occasional apparition; and indeed the novel has no hero, but only a heroine.

The same remark applies to *Adam Bede,*

as the work stands. The central figure of the book, by virtue of her great misfortune, is Hetty Sorrel. In the presence of that misfortune no one else, assuredly, has a right to claim dramatic pre-eminence. The one person for whom an approach to equality may be claimed is, not Adam Bede, but Arthur Donnithorne. If the story had ended, as I should have infinitely preferred to see it end, with Hetty's execution, or even with her reprieve, and if Adam had been left to his grief, and Dinah Morris to the enjoyment of that distinguished celibacy for which she was so well suited, then I think Adam might have shared the honours of pre-eminence with his hapless sweetheart. But as it is, the continuance of the book in his interest is fatal to him. His sorrow at Hetty's misfortune is not a *sufficient* sorrow for the situation. That his marriage at some future time was quite possible, and even natural, I readily admit; but that was matter for a new story.

This point illustrates, I think, the great advantage of the much-censured method, introduced by Balzac, of continuing his heroes' adventures from tale to tale. Or, admitting that the author was indisposed to undertake, or even to conceive, in its completeness, a new tale, in which Adam, healed of his wound by time, should address himself to another woman, I yet hold that it would be possible tacitly to foreshadow some such event at the close of the tale which we are supposing to end with Hetty's death,—to make it the logical consequence of Adam's final state of mind. Of course circumstances would have much to do with bringing it to pass, and these circumstances could not be foreshadowed; but apart from the action of circumstances would stand the fact that, to begin with, the event was *possible*.

The assurance of this possibility is what I should have desired the author to place the sympathetic reader at a stand-point to deduce for himself. In every novel the work is divided between the writer and the reader; but the writer makes the reader very much as he makes his characters. When he makes him ill, that is, makes him different, he does no work; the writer does all. When he makes him well, that is, makes him interested, then the reader does quite half the labour. In making such a deduction as I have just indicated, the reader would be doing but his share of the task; the grand point is to get him to make it. I hold that there is a way. It is perhaps a secret; but until it is found out, I think the art of story-telling cannot be said to have approached perfection. . . .

My chief complaint with Adam Bede himself is that he is too good. He is meant, I conceive, to be every inch a man; but, to my mind, there are several inches wanting. He lacks spontaneity and sensibility, he is too stiff-backed. He lacks that supreme quality without which a man can never be interesting to men,—the capacity to be tempted. His nature is without richness or responsiveness. I doubt not that such men as he exist, especially in the author's thrice-English Loamshire; she has partially described them as a class, with a felicity which carries conviction. She claims for her hero that, although a plain man, he was as little an ordinary man as he was a genius. . . .

About Hetty Sorrel I shall have no hesitation whatever: I accept her with all my heart. Of all George Eliot's female figures she is the least ambitious, and on the whole, I think, the most successful. The part of the story which concerns her is much the most forcible; and there is something infinitely tragic in the reader's sense of the contrast between the sternly prosaic life of the good people about her, their wholesome decency and their noonday probity, and the dusky sylvan path along which poor Hetty is tripping, light-footed, to her ruin. Hetty's conduct throughout seems to me to be thoroughly consistent. The author has escaped the easy error of representing her as in any degree made serious by suffering. She is vain and superficial by nature; and she remains so to the end. . . .

It is not in her conceptions nor her composition that George Eliot is strongest: it is in her *touches.* In these she is quite original. She is a good deal of a humourist, and something of a satirist; but she is neither Dickens nor Thackeray. She has over them the great advantage that she is also a good deal of a philosopher; and it is to this union of the keenest observation with the ripest reflection, that her style owes its essential force. She is a thinker,—not, perhaps, a passionate thinker, but at least a serious one; and the term can be applied with either adjective neither to Dickens nor Thackeray. The constant play of lively and vigourous thought about the objects furnished by her observation animates these latter with a surprising richness of colour and a truly human interest. It gives to the author's style, moreover, that lingering, affectionate, comprehensive quality which is its chief distinction; and perhaps occasionally it makes her tedious. George Eliot is so little tedious, however, because, if, on the one hand, her reflection never flags, so, on the other, her observation never ceases to supply it with material. Her observation, I think, is decidedly of the feminine kind: it deals, in preference, with small things. This fact may be held to explain the excellence of what I have called her pictures, and the comparative feebleness of her dramatic movement. . . .

Of the four English stories, *The Mill on the Floss* seems to me to have most dramatic continuity, in distinction from that descriptive, discursive method of narration which I have attempted to indicate. After Hetty Sorrel, I think Maggie Tulliver the most successful of the author's young women, and after Tito Melema, Tom Tulliver the best of her young men. English novels abound in pictures of childhood; but I know of none more truthful and touching than the early pages of this work. Poor erratic Maggie is worth a hundred of her positive brother, and yet on the very threshold of life she is compelled to accept him as her master. He falls naturally into the man's privilege of always being in the right. . . .

The chief defect—indeed, the only serious one—in *The Mill on the Floss* is its conclusion. Such a conclusion is in itself assuredly not illegitimate, and there is nothing in the fact of the flood, to my knowledge, essentially unnatural: what I object to is its relation to the preceding part of the story. The story is told as if it were destined to have, if not a strictly happy termination, at least one within ordinary probabilities. As it stands, the *dénouement* shocks the reader most painfully. Nothing has prepared him for it; the story does not move towards it; it casts no shadow before it. Did such a *dénouement* lie within the author's intentions from the first, or was it a tardy expedient for the solution of Maggie's difficulties? This question the reader asks himself, but of course he asks it in vain.

For my part, although, as long as humanity is subject to floods and earthquakes, I have no objection to see them made use of in novels, I would in this particular case have infinitely preferred that Maggie should have been left to her own devices. I understand the author's scruples, and to a certain degree I respect them. A lonely spinsterhood seemed but a dismal consummation of her generous life; and yet, as the author conceives, it was unlikely that she would return to Stephen Guest. I respect Maggie profoundly; but nevertheless I ask, Was this after all so unlikely? I will not try to answer the question. I have shown enough courage in asking it. But one thing is certain: a *dénouement* by which Maggie should have called Stephen back would have been extremely interesting, and would have had far more in its favour than can be put to confusion by a mere exclamation of horror.

I have come to the end of my space without speaking of *Romola*, which, as the most important of George Eliot's works, I had kept in reserve. I have only room to say that on the whole I think it *is* decidedly

the most important,—not the most entertaining nor the most readable, but the one in which the largest things are attempted and grasped. The figure of Savonarola, subordinate though it is, is a figure on a larger scale than any which George Eliot has elsewhere undertaken; and in the career of Tito Melema there is a fuller representation of the development of a character.

Considerable as are our author's qualities as an artist, and largely as they are displayed in "Romola," the book strikes me less as a work of art than as a work of morals. Like all of George Eliot's works, its dramatic construction is feeble; the story drags and halts,—the setting is too large for the picture; but I remember that, the first time I read it, I declared to myself that much should be forgiven it for the sake of its generous feeling and its elevated morality. I still recognize this latter fact, but I think I find it more on a level than I at first found it with the artistic conditions of the book. . . .

One word more. Of all the impressions —and they are numerous—which a reperusal of George Eliot's writings has given me, I find the strongest to be this: that (with all deference to *Felix Holt, the Radical*) the author is in morals and æsthetics essentially a conservative. In morals her problems are still the old, passive problems. I use the word "old" with all respect. What moves her most is the idea of a conscience harassed by the memory of slighted obligations. Unless in the case of Savonarola, she has made no attempt to depict a conscience taking upon itself great and novel responsibilities. In her last work, assuredly such an attempt was—considering the title—conspicuous by its absence.

Of a corresponding tendency in the second department of her literary character,— or perhaps I should say in a certain middle field where morals and æsthetics move in concert,—it is very difficult to give an example. A tolerably good one is furnished by her inclination to compromise with the

Henry James

old tradition—and here I use the word "old" *without* respect—which exacts that a serious story of manners shall close with the factitious happiness of a fairy-tale. I know few things more irritating in a literary way than each of her final chapters,— for even in *The Mill on the Floss* there is a fatal "Conclusion." Both as an artist and a thinker, in other words, our author is an optimist; and although a conservative is not necessarily an optimist, I think an optimist is pretty likely to be a conservative.

Henry James

The Life of George Eliot

. . . The fault of most of her work is the absence of spontaneity, the excess of reflection; and by her action in 1854 (which seemed superficially to be of the sort usually termed reckless), she committed herself to being nothing if not reflective, to cultivating a kind of compensatory earnestness. Her earnestness, her educated conscience, her exalted sense of responsibility, were coloured by her peculiar position; they committed her to a plan of life, of study, in which the accidental, the unexpected, were too little allowed for, and this is what I mean by speaking of her sequestration. If her relations with the world had been easier, in a word, her books would have been less difficult. . . .

It is striking that from the first her conception of the novelist's task is never in the least as the game of art. The most interesting passage in Mr. Cross's volumes is to my sense a simple sentence in a short entry in her journal in the year 1859, just after she had finished the first volume of *The Mill on the Floss* (the original title of which, by the way, had been *Sister Maggie*): "We have just finished reading aloud Père Goriot, a hateful book." That Balzac's masterpiece should have elicited from her only this remark, at a time, too, when her mind might have been opened to it by her own activity of composition, is significant of so many things that the few words are, in the whole *Life*, those I should have been most sorry to lose. Of course they are not all George Eliot would have had to say about Balzac, if some other occasion than a simple jotting in a diary had presented itself. Still, what even a jotting may *not* have said after a first perusal of *Le Père* Goriot is eloquent; it illuminates the author's general attitude with regard to the novel, which, for her, was not primarily a picture of life, capable of deriving a high value from its form, but a moralised fable, the last word of a philosophy endeavouring to teach by example.

This is a very noble and defensible view, and one must speak respectfully of any theory of work which would produce such fruit as *Romola* and *Middlemarch*. But it testifies to that side of George Eliot's nature which was weakest—the absence of free æsthetic life (I venture this remark in the face of a passage quoted from one of her letters in Mr. Cross's third volume); it gives the hand, as it were, to several other instances that may be found in the same pages. "My function is that of the *æsthetic*, not the doctrinal teacher; the rousing of the nobler emotions, which make mankind desire the social right, not the prescribing of special measures, concerning which the artistic mind, however strongly moved by social sympathy, is often not the best judge." That is the passage referred to in my parenthetic allusion, and it is a good general description of the manner in which George Eliot may be said to have acted on her generation; but the "artistic mind," the possession of which it implies, existed in her with limitations remarkable in a writer whose imagination was so rich. We feel in her, always, that she proceeds from the abstract to the concrete; that her figures and situations are evolved, as the phrase is, from her moral consciousness, and are only indirectly the products of observation. They are deeply studied and massively supported, but they are not *seen*, in the irresponsible

First printed in the *Atlantic Monthly* in 1885; reprinted in *Partial Portraits*, London, Macmillan, 1888.

plastic way. The world was, first and foremost, for George Eliot, the moral, the intellectual world; the personal spectacle came after; and lovingly humanly as she regarded it we constantly feel that she cares for the things she finds in it only so far as they are types. The philosophic door is always open, on her stage, and we are aware that the somewhat cooling draught of ethical purpose draws across it. This constitutes half the beauty of her work; the constant reference to ideas may be an excellent source of one kind of reality—for, after all, the secret of seeing a thing well is not necessarily that you see nothing else. Her preoccupation with the universe helped to make her characters strike you as also belonging to it; it raised the roof, widened the area, of her æsthetic structure. Nothing is finer, in her genius, than the combination of her love of general truth and love of the special case; without this, indeed, we should not have heard of her as a novelist, for the passion of the special case is surely the basis of the story-teller's art. All the same, that little sign of all that Balzac failed to suggest to her showed at what perils the special case got itself considered. Such dangers increased as her activity proceeded, and many judges perhaps hold that in her ultimate work, in *Middlemarch* and *Daniel Deronda* (especially the latter), it ceased to be considered at all. Such critics assure us that Gwendolen and Grandcourt, Deronda and Myra, are not concrete images, but disembodied types, pale abstractions, signs and symbols of a "great lesson." I give up Deronda and Myra to the objector, but Grandcourt and Gwendolen seem to me to have a kind of superior reality; to be, in a high degree, what one demands of a figure in a novel, planted on their legs and complete.

The truth is, perception and reflection, at the outset, divided George Eliot's great talent between them; but as time went on circumstances led the latter to develop itself at the expense of the former—one of these circumstances being apparently the influence of George Henry Lewes. Lewes was interested in science, in cosmic problems; and though his companion, thanks to the original bent of her versatile, powerful mind, needed no impulse from without to turn herself to speculation, yet the contagion of his studies pushed her further than she would otherwise have gone in the direction of scientific observation, which is but another form of what I have called reflection. Her early novels are full of natural as distinguished from systematic observation, though even in them it is less the dominant note, I think, than the love of the "moral," the reaction of thought in the face of the human comedy. They had observation sufficient, at any rate, to make their fortune, and it may well be said that that is enough for any novel. In *Silas Marner,* in *Adam Bede,* the quality seems gilded by a sort of autumn haze, an afternoon light, of meditation, which mitigates the sharpness of portraiture. I doubt very much whether the author herself had a clear vision, for instance, of the marriage of Dinah Morris to Adam, or of the rescue of Hetty from the scaffold at the eleventh hour. The reason of this may be, indeed, that her perception was a perception of nature much more than of art, and that these particular incidents do not belong to nature (to my sense at least); by which I do not mean that they belong to a very happy art. I cite them, on the contrary, as an evidence of artistic weakness; they are a very good example of the view in which a story must have marriages and rescues in the nick of time, as a matter of course. I must add, in fairness to George Eliot, that the marriage of the nun-like Dinah, which shocks the reader, who sees in it a base concession, was a *trouvaille* of Lewes's and is a small sign of that same faulty judgment in literary things which led him to throw his influence on the side of her writing verse— verse which is *all* reflection, with direct, vivifying vision, or emotion, remarkably absent. . . .

It was in *Romola,* precisely, that the equilibrium I spoke of just now was lost,

Discussions of George Eliot

and that reflection began to weigh down the scale. *Romola* is preeminently a study of the human conscience in an historical setting which is studied almost as much, and few passages in Mr. Cross's volumes are more interesting than those relating to the production of this magnificent romance. George Eliot took all her work with a noble seriousness, but into none of it did she throw herself with more passion. It drained from her as much as she gave to it; and none of her writing ploughed into her, to use her biographer's expression, so deeply. She told him that she began it a young woman and finished it an old one. More than any of her novels it was evolved, as I have said, from her moral consciousness encircled by a prodigious amount of literary research. Her literary ideal was at all times of the highest, but in the preparation of *Romola* it placed her under a control absolutely religious. She read innumerable books, some of them bearing only remotely on her subject, and consulted without stint contemporary records and documents. She neglected nothing that would enable her to live, intellectually, in the period she had undertaken to describe. We know, for the most part, I think, the result. *Romola* is on the whole the finest thing she wrote, but its defects are almost on the scale of its beauties. The great defect is that, except in the person of Tito Melema, it does not seem positively to live. It is overladen with learning, it smells of the lamp, it tastes just perceptibly of pedantry. In spite of its want of blood, however, it assuredly will survive in men's remembrance, for the finest pages in it belong to the finest part of our literature. It is on the whole a failure, but such a failure as only a great talent can produce; and one may say of it that there are many great "hits" far less interesting than such a mistake. A twentieth part of the erudition would have sufficed, would have given us the feeling and colour of the time, if there had been more of the breath of the Florentine streets, more of the faculty of optical evocation, a greater satu-

ration of the senses with the elements of the adorable little city. The difficulty with the book, for the most part, is that it is not Italian; it has always seemed to me the most Germanic of the author's productions. I cannot imagine a German writing (in the way of a novel) anything half so good; but if I could imagine it I should suppose *Romola* to be very much the sort of picture he would achieve—the sort of medium through which he would show us how, by the Arnoside, the fifteenth century came to an end. One of the sources of interest in the book is that, more than any of its companions, it indicates how much George Eliot proceeded by reflection and research; how little important, comparatively, she thought that same breath of the streets. It carries to a maximum the in-door quality.

The most definite impression produced, perhaps, by Mr. Cross's volumes (by the second and third) is that of simple success —success which had been the result of no external accidents (unless her union with Lewes be so denominated), but was involved in the very faculties nature had given her. All the elements of an eventual happy fortune met in her constitution. The great foundation, to begin with, was there —the magnificent mind, vigorous, luminous, and eminently sane. To her intellectual vigour, her immense facility, her exemption from cerebral lassitude, her letters and journals bear the most copious testimony. Her daily stint of arduous reading and writing was of the largest. Her ability, as one may express it in the most general way, was astonishing, and it belonged to every season of her long and fruitful career. Her passion for study encountered no impediment, but was able to make everything feed and support it. The extent and variety of her knowledge is by itself the measure of a capacity which triumphed wherever it wished. Add to this an immense special talent which, as soon as it tries its wings, is found to be adequate to the highest, longest flights and brings back great material rewards. George Eliot of course had drawbacks and difficulties, physical infirmities, constant liabilities to headache, dyspepsia, and other illness, to deep depression, to despair about her work; but these jolts of the chariot were small in proportion to the impetus acquired, and were hardly greater than was necessary for reminding her of the secret of all ambitious workers in the field of art—that effort, effort, always effort, is the only key to success. Her great furtherance was that, intensely intellectual being as she was, the life of affection and emotion was also widely open to her. She had all the initiation of knowledge and none of its dryness, all the advantages of judgment and all the luxuries of feeling. She had an imagination which enabled her to sit at home with book and pen, and yet enter into the life of other generations; project herself into Warwickshire alehouses and Florentine symposia, reconstitute conditions utterly different from her own. Toward the end she triumphed over the great impossible; she reconciled the greatest sensibility with the highest serenity. She succeeded in guarding her pursuits from intrusion; in carrying out her habits; in sacrificing her work as little as possible; in leading, in the midst of a society united in conspiracies to interrupt and vulgarise, an independent, strenuously personal life. People who had the honour of penetrating into the sequestered precinct of the Priory —the house in London in which she lived from 1863 to 1880—remember well a kind of sanctity in the place, an atmosphere of stillness and concentration, something that suggested a literary temple. . . .

There is one question we cannot help asking ourselves as we close this record of her life; it is impossible not to let our imagination wander in the direction of what turn her mind or her fortune might have taken if she had never met George Henry Lewes, or never cast her lot with his. It is safe to say that, in one way or another, in the long run, her novels would have got themselves written, and it is possible they would have been more natural, as one may call it, more familiarly and casually human. Would her development have been less systematic, more irresponsible, more personal, and should we have had more of *Adam Bede* and *Silas Marner* and less of *Romola* and *Middlemarch?* The question, after all, cannot be answered, and I do not push it, being myself very grateful for *Middlemarch* and *Romola*. It is as George Eliot does actually present herself that we must judge her—a condition that will not prevent her from striking us as one of the noblest, most beautiful minds of our time. This impression bears the reader company throughout these letters and notes. It is impossible not to feel, as we close them, that she was an admirable being. They are less brilliant, less entertaining, than we might have hoped; they contain fewer "good things" and have even a certain grayness of tone, something measured and subdued, as of a person talking without ever raising her voice. But there rises from them a kind of fragrance of moral elevation; a love of justice, truth, and light; a large, generous way of looking at things; and a constant effort to hold high the torch in the dusky spaces of man's conscience. That is how we see her during the latter years of her life: frail, delicate, shivering a little, much fatigued and considerably spent, but still meditating on what could be acquired and imparted; still living, in the intelligence, a freer, larger life than probably had ever been the portion of any woman. To her own sex her memory, her example, will remain of the highest value; those of them for whom the "development" of woman is the hope of the future ought to erect a monument to George Eliot. She helped on the cause more than any one, in proving how few limitations are of necessity implied in the feminine organism. She went so far that such a distance seems enough, and in her effort she sacrificed no tenderness, no grace. There is much talk to-day about things being "open to women"; but George Eliot showed that there is nothing that is closed. If we criticise her novels we must remember that her nature came first and her work afterwards, and that it is not remarkable they should not resemble the productions, say, of Alexandre Dumas. What *is* remarkable, extraordinary—and the process remains inscrutable and mysterious—is that this quiet, anxious, sedentary, serious, invalidical English lady, without animal spirits, without adventures or sensations, should have made us believe that nothing in the world was alien to her; should have produced such rich, deep, masterly pictures of the multiform life of man.

Henry James

Morals - Theodora [Dorothea
Pulcheria - Artistic; Beautiful
Constantius - Considering

Daniel Deronda: A Conversation

. . . *Constantius.* I have been wanting to say that there seems to me to be two very distinct elements in George Eliot—a spontaneous one and an artificial one. There is what she is by inspiration and what she is because it is expected of her. These two heads have been very perceptible in her recent writings; they are much less noticeable in her early ones.

Theodora. You mean that she is too scientific? So long as she remains the great literary genius that she is, how can she be too scientific? She is simply permeated with the highest culture of the age.

Pulcheria. She talks too much about the "dynamic quality" of people's eyes. When she uses such a phrase as that in the first sentence in her book she is not a great literary genius, because she shows a want of tact. There can't be a worse limitation.

Constantius. The "dynamic quality" of Gwendolen's glance has made the tour of the world.

Theodora. It shows a very low level of culture on the world's part to be agitated by a term perfectly familiar to all decently-educated people.

Pulcheria. I don't pretend to be decently educated; pray tell me what it means.

Constantius (promptly). I think Pulcheria has hit it in speaking of a want of tact. In the manner of the book, throughout, there is something that one may call a want of tact. The epigraphs in verse are a want of tact; they are sometimes, I think, a trifle more pretentious than really pregnant; the importunity of the moral reflections is a want of tact; the very diffuseness is a want of tact. But it comes back to what I said just now about one's sense of the author writing under a sort of external pressure.

From *Partial Portraits*, London, Macmillan, 1888.

I began to notice it in *Felix Holt*; I don't think I had before. She strikes me as a person who certainly has naturally a taste for general considerations, but who has fallen upon an age and a circle which have compelled her to give them an exaggerated attention. She does not strike me as naturally a critic, less still as naturally a sceptic; her spontaneous part is to observe life and to feel it, to feel it with admirable depth. Contemplation, sympathy and faith—something like that, I should say, would have been her natural scale. If she had fallen upon an age of enthusiastic assent to old articles of faith, it seems to me possible that she would have had a more perfect, a more consistent and graceful development, than she has actually had. If she had cast herself into such a current—her genius being equal—it might have carried her to splendid distances. But she has chosen to go into criticism, and to the critics she addresses her work; I mean the critics of the universe. Instead of feeling life itself, it is "views" upon life that she tries to feel.

Pulcheria. She is the victim of a first-class education. I am so glad!

Constantius. Thanks to her admirable intellect she philosophises very sufficiently; but meanwhile she has given a chill to her genius. She has come near spoiling an artist.

Pulcheria. She has quite spoiled one. Or rather I shouldn't say that, because there was no artist to spoil. I maintain that she is not an artist. An artist could never have put a story together so monstrously ill. She has no sense of form.

Theodora. Pray, what could be more artistic than the way that Deronda's paternity is concealed till almost the end, and

14   Discussions of George Eliot

the way we are made to suppose Sir Hugo is his father?

Pulcheria. And Mirah his sister. How does that fit together? I was as little made to suppose he was not a Jew as I cared when I found out he was. And his mother popping up through a trap-door and popping down again, at the last, in that scrambling fashion! His mother is very bad.

Constantius. I think Deronda's mother is one of the unvivified characters; she belongs to the cold half of the book. All the Jewish part is at bottom cold; that is my only objection. I have enjoyed it because my fancy often warms cold things; but beside Gwendolen's history it is like the empty half of the lunar disk beside the full one. It is admirably studied, it is imagined, it is understood, but it is not embodied. One feels this strongly in just those scenes between Deronda and his mother; one feels that one has been appealed to on rather an artificial ground of interest. To make Deronda's reversion to his native faith more dramatic and profound, the author has given him a mother who on very arbitrary grounds, apparently, has separated herself from this same faith and who has been kept waiting in the wing, as it were, for many acts, to come on and make her speech and say so. This moral situation of hers we are invited retrospectively to appreciate. But we hardly care to do so.

Pulcheria. I don't *see* the princess, in spite of her flame-coloured robe. Why should an actress and prima-donna care so much about religious matters?

Theodora. It was not only that; it was the Jewish race she hated, Jewish manners and looks. You, my dear, ought to understand that.

Pulcheria. I do, but I am not a Jewish actress of genius; I am not what Rachel was. If I were I should have other things to think about.

Constantius. Think now a little about poor Gwendolen.

Pulcheria. I don't care to think about her. She was a second-rate English girl who got into a flutter about a lord.

Theodora. I don't see that she is worse than if she were a first-rate American girl who should get into exactly the same flutter.

Pulcheria. It wouldn't be the same flutter at all; it wouldn't be any flutter. She wouldn't be afraid of the lord, though she might be amused at him.

Theodora. I am sure I don't perceive whom Gwendolen was afraid of. She was afraid of her misdeed—her broken promise —after she had committed it, and through that fear she was afraid of her husband. Well she might be! I can imagine nothing more vivid than the sense we get of his absolutely clammy selfishness.

Pulcheria. She was not afraid of Deronda when, immediately after her marriage and without any but the most casual acquaintance with him, she begins to hover about him at the Mallingers' and to drop little confidences about her conjugal woes. That seems to me very indelicate; ask any woman.

Constantius. The very purpose of the author is to give us an idea of the sort of confidence that *Deronda* inspired—its irresistible potency.

Pulcheria. A lay father-confessor— horrid!

Constantius. And to give us an idea also of the acuteness of Gwendolen's depression, of her haunting sense of impending trouble.

Theodora. It must be remembered that Gwendolen was in love with Deronda from the first, long before she knew it. She didn't know it, poor girl, but that was it.

Pulcheria. That makes the matter worse. It is very disagreeable to see her hovering and rustling about a man who is indifferent to her.

Theodora. He was not indifferent to her, since he sent her back her necklace.

Pulcheria. Of all the delicate attention to a charming girl that I ever heard of, that little pecuniary transaction is the most felicitous.

Constantius. You must remember that he had been *en rapport* with her at the gaming-table. She had been playing in defiance of his observation, and he, continuing to observe her, had been in a measure responsible for her loss. There was a tacit consciousness of this between them. You may contest the possibility of tacit consciousness going so far, but that is not a serious objection. You may point out two or three weak spots in detail; the fact remains that Gwendolen's whole history is vividly told. And see how the girl is known, inside out, how thoroughly she is felt and understood. It is the most *intelligent* thing in all George Eliot's writing, and that is saying much. It is so deep, so true, so complete, it holds such a wealth of psychological detail, it is more than masterly.

Theodora. I don't know where the perception of character has sailed closer to the wind.

Pulcheria. The portrait may be admirable, but it has one little fault. You don't care a straw for the original. Gwendolen is not an interesting girl, and when the author tries to invest her with a deep tragic interest she does so at the expense of consistency. She has made her at the outset too light, too flimsy; tragedy has no hold on such a girl.

Theodora. You are hard to satisfy. You said this morning that Dorothea was too heavy, and now you find Gwendolen too light. George Eliot wished to give us the perfect counterpart of Dorothea. Having made one portrait she was worthy to make the other.

Pulcheria. She has committed the fatal error of making Gwendolen vulgarly, pettily, drily selfish. She was *personally* selfish.

Theodora. I know nothing more personal than selfishness.

Pulcheria. I am selfish, but I don't go about with my chin out like that; at least I hope I don't. She was an odious young woman, and one can't care what becomes of her. When her marriage turned out ill she would have become still more hard and positive; to make her soft and appealing is very bad logic. The second Gwendolen doesn't belong to the first.

Constantius. She is perhaps at the first a little childish for the weight of interest she has to carry, a little too much after the pattern of the unconscientious young ladies of Miss Yonge and Miss Sewell.

Theodora. Since when is it forbidden to make one's heroine young? Gwendolen is a perfect picture of youthfulness—its eagerness, its presumption, its preoccupation with itself, its vanity and silliness, its sense of its own absoluteness. But she is extremely intelligent and clever, and therefore tragedy *can* have a hold upon her. Her conscience doesn't make the tragedy; that is an old story and, I think, a secondary form of suffering. It is the tragedy that makes her conscience, which then reacts upon it; and I can think of nothing more powerful than the way in which the growth of her conscience is traced, nothing more touching than the picture of its helpless maturity.

Constantius. That is perfectly true. Gwendolen's history is admirably typical—as most things are with George Eliot: it is the very stuff that human life is made of. What is it made of but the discovery by each of us that we are at the best but a rather ridiculous fifth wheel to the coach, after we have sat cracking our whip and believing that we are at least the coachman in person? We think we are the main hoop to the barrel, and we turn out to be but a very incidental splinter in one of the staves. The universe forcing itself with a slow, inexorable pressure into a narrow, complacent, and yet after all extremely sensitive mind, and making it ache with the pain of the process—that is Gwendolen's story. And it becomes completely characteristic in that her supreme perception of the fact that the world is whirling past her is in the disappointment not of a base but of an exalted passion. The very chance to embrace what the author is so fond of calling a "larger life" seems refused to her. She is punished for being narrow, and she is not allowed a chance to expand. Her finding Deronda preengaged to go to the East and stir up the race-feeling of the Jews strikes me as a wonderfully happy invention. The irony of the situation, for poor Gwendolen, is almost grotesque, and it makes one wonder whether the whole heavy structure of the Jewish question in the story was not built up by the author for the express purpose of giving its proper force to this particular stroke.

Theodora. George Eliot's intentions are extremely complex. The mass is for each detail and each detail is for the mass.

Pulcheria. She is very fond of deaths by drowning. Maggie Tulliver and her brother are drowned, Tito Melema is drowned, Mr. Grandcourt is drowned. It is extremely unlikely that Grandcourt should not have known how to swim.

Constantius. He did, of course, but he had a cramp. It served him right. I can't imagine a more consummate representation of the most detestable kind of Englishman —the Englishman who thinks it low to articulate. And in Grandcourt the type and the individual are so happily met: the type with its sense of the proprieties and the individual with his absence of all sense. He is the apotheosis of dryness, a human expression of the simple idea of the perpendicular.

Theodora. Mr. Casaubon, in *Middlemarch*, was very dry too; and yet what a genius it is that can give us two disagreeable husbands who are so utterly different!

Pulcheria. You must count the two disagreeable wives too—Rosamond Vincy and Gwendolen. They are very much alike. I know the author didn't mean it; it proves how common a type the worldly, *pincée*, selfish young woman seemed to her. They are both disagreeable; you can't get over that.

Constantius. There is something in that, perhaps. I think, at any rate, that the secondary people here are less delightful than in *Middlemarch;* there is nothing so good as Mary Garth and her father, or the little old lady who steals sugar, or the parson who is in love with Mary, or the country relatives of old Mr. Featherstone. Rex Gascoigne is not so good as Fred Vincy.

Theodora. Mr. Gascoigne is admirable, and Mrs. Davilow is charming.

Pulcheria. And you must not forget that you think Herr Klesmer "Shakespearean." Wouldn't "Wagnerian" be high enough praise?

Constantius. Yes, one must make an exception with regard to the Klesmers and the Meyricks. They are delightful, and as for Klesmer himself, and Hans Meyrick, Theodora may maintain her epithet. Shakespearean characters are characters that are born of the *overflow* of observation—characters that make the drama seem multitudinous, like life. Klesmer comes in with a sort of Shakespearean "value," as a painter would say, and so, in a different tone, does Hans Meyrick. They spring from a much-peopled mind.

Theodora. I think Gwendolen's confrontation with Klesmer one of the finest things in the book.

Constantius. It is like everything in George Eliot; it will bear thinking of.

Pulcheria. All that is very fine, but you cannot persuade me that *Deronda* is not a very ponderous and ill-made story. It has nothing that one can call a subject. A silly young girl and a solemn, sapient young man who doesn't fall in love with her! That is the *donnée* of eight monthly volumes. I call it very flat. Is that what the exquisite art of Thackeray and Miss Austen and Hawthorne has come to? I would as soon read a German novel outright.

Theodora. There is something higher than form—there is spirit.

Constantius. I am afraid Pulcheria is sadly æsthetic. She had better confine herself to Mérimée.

Pulcheria. I shall certainly to-day read over *La Double Méprise.*

Theodora. Oh, my dear, *y pensez-vous?*

Constantius. Yes, I think there is little art in *Deronda*, but I think there is a vast amount of life. In life without art you can find your account; but art without life is a poor affair. The book is full of the world.

Leslie Stephen

George Eliot

HAD we been asked, a few weeks ago, to name the greatest living writer of English fiction, the answer would have been unanimous. No one—whatever might be his special personal predilections—would have refused that title to George Eliot. To ask the same question now would be to suggest some measure of our loss. In losing George Eliot we have probably lost the greatest woman who ever won literary fame, and one of the very few writers of our day to whom the name "great" could be conceded with any plausibility. . . .

Hardly any great English writer has left a greater quantity of work representing the highest level of the author's capacity than is equivalent to the "Scenes of Clerical Life," "Adam Bede," the "Mill on the Floss," "Silas Marner," "Romola," and "Middlemarch." Certainly, she might have done more. She did not begin to write novels till a period at which many popular authors are already showing symptoms of exhaustion, and indulging in the perilous practice of self-imitation. Why, it may be said, did not George Eliot write immortal works in her youth, instead of translating German authors of a heterodox tendency? If we could arrange all such things to our taste, and could foresee a writer's powers from the beginning, we might have ordered matters differently. Yet one may observe that there is another side to the question. Imaginative minds often ripen quickly; and much of the finest poetry in the language derives its charm from the freshness of youth. But writers of the contemplative order—those whose best works represent the general experience of a rich and

thoughtful nature—may be expected to come later to their maturity. The phenomenon of early exhaustion is too common in these days to allow us to regret an occasional exception. If during her youth George Eliot was storing the thoughts and emotions which afterwards shaped themselves into the "Scenes of Clerical Life," we need not suppose that the time was wasted. Certainly, I do not think that anyone who has had a little experience in such matters would regard it as otherwise than dangerous for a powerful mind to be precipitated into public utterance. The Pythagorean probation of silence may be protracted too long; but it may afford a most useful discipline: and I think that there is nothing preposterous in the supposition that George Eliot's work was all the more powerful because it came from a novelist who had lain fallow through a longer period than ordinary. . . .

The poor woman was not content simply to write amusing stories. She is convicted upon conclusive evidence of having indulged in ideas; she ventured to speculate upon human life and its meaning, and still worse, she endeavoured to embody her convictions in imaginative shapes, and probably wished to infect her readers with them. This was, according to some people, highly unbecoming in a woman and very inartistic in a novelist. I confess that, for my part, I am rather glad to find ideas anywhere. They are not very common; and there are a vast number of excellent fictions which these sensitive critics may study without the least danger of a shock to their artistic sensibilities by anything of the kind. But

First printed in the *Cornhill Magazine* in 1881; reprinted in *Hours in a Library*, London, Smith, Elder & Company, 1892.

Discussions of George Eliot

if you will permit a poor novelist to indulge in such awkward possessions, I cannot see why he or she should not be allowed occasionally to interweave them in her narrative, taking care of course to keep them in their proper place. Some of that mannerism which offends many critics represents in fact simply George Eliot's way of using this privilege. We are indeed told dogmatically that a novelist should never indulge in little asides to the reader. Why not? One main advantage of a novel, as it seems to me, is precisely that it leaves room for a freedom in such matters which is incompatible with the requirements, for example, of dramatic writing. I can enjoy Scott's downright story-telling, which never reminds you obtrusively of the presence of the author; but with all respect for Scott, I do not see why his manner should be the sole type and model for all his successors. I like to read about Tom Jones or Colonel Newcome; but I am also very glad when Fielding or Thackeray puts his puppets aside for the moment and talks to me in his own person. A child, it is true, dislikes to have the illusion broken, and is angry if you try to persuade him that Giant Despair was not a real personage like his favourite Blunderbore. But the attempt to produce such illusions is really unworthy of work intended for full-grown readers. The humourist in particular knows that you will not mistake his puppet-show for reality, nor does he wish you to do so. He is rather of opinion that the world itself is a greater puppet-show, not to be taken in too desperate earnest. It is congenial to his whole mode of thought to act occasionally as chorus, and dwell upon some incidental suggestion. The solemn critic may step forward, like the physician who attended Sancho Panza's meal, and waive aside the condiment which gives a peculiar relish to the feast. It is not prepared according to his recipe. But till he gives me some better reason for obedience than his *ipse dixit*, I shall refuse to respect what would destroy many charming passages and obliterate

touches which clearly contribute to the general effect of George Eliot's work. . . .

George Eliot's early books owe their charm to the exquisite painting of the old country-life—an achievement made possible by a tender imagination brooding over a vanishing past—but, if we may make the distinction, they owe their greatness to the insight into passions not confined to one race or period. Janet Dempster would lose much of her charm if she were transplanted from Milby to London; but she would still be profoundly interesting as representing a marked type of feminine character. Balzac—or somebody else—said, or is said to have said, that there were only seven possible plots in fiction. Without pledging oneself to the particular number, one may admit that the number of radically different motives is remarkably small. It may be added that even great writers rarely show their highest capacity in more than one of these typical situations. It is not hard to say which is George Eliot's favourite theme. We may call it—speaking with proper reserve—the woman in need of a confessor. We may have the comparatively shallow nature, the poor wilful little Tina, or Hetty or Tessa—the mere plaything of fate, whom we pity because in her childish ignorance she is apt, like little Red Ridinghood, to mistake the wolf for a friend, though not exactly to take him for a grandmother. Or we have the woman with noble aspirations—Janet, or Dinah, or Maggie, or Romola, or Dorothea, or—may we add?—Daniel Deronda, who recognises more clearly her own need of guidance, and even in failure has the lofty air of martyrdom. It is in the setting such characters before us that George Eliot has achieved her highest triumphs, and made some of her most unmistakable failures. It is here that we meet the complaint that she is too analytic; that she takes the point of view of the confessor rather than the artist; and is more anxious to probe the condition of her heroines' souls, to give us an accurate diagnosis of their spiritual complaints, and an account of their moral evolution, than to show us the character in action. If I must give my own view, I must venture a distinction. To say that George Eliot's stories are interesting as studies of human nature, is really to say little more than that they deserve serious attention. There are stories —and very excellent and amusing stories— which have comparatively little to do with character; histories of wondrous and moving events, where you are fascinated by the vivacity of the narrator without caring much for the passions of the actors—such stories, in fact, as compose the Arabian Nights, or the voluminous works of the admirable Alexandre Dumas. We do not care to understand Aladdin's sentiments, or to say how far he differed from Sinbad and Camaralzaman. The famous Musketeers have different parts to play, and so far different characters; but one does not care very much for their psychology. Still, every serious writer must derive his power from his insight into men and women. A Cervantes or Shakespeare, a Scott, a Fielding, a Richardson or Thackeray, command our attention by forcible presentation of certain types of character; and, so far, George Eliot's does not differ from her predecessors'. Nor, again, would any truly imaginative writer give us mere abstract analyses of character, instead of showing us the concrete person in action. If George Eliot has a tendency to this error, it does not appear in her early period. We can see any of her best characters as distinctly, we know them by direct vision as intimately, as we know any personage in real or fictitious history. We are not put off with the formulæ of their conduct, but persons are themselves revealed to us. Yet it is, I think, true that her stories are preeminently studies of character in the sense, that her main and conscious purpose is to set before us the living beings in what may be called, with due apology, their statical relations—to show them, that is, in their quiet and normal state, not under the stress of exceptional events. When we once know

Adam Bede or Dinah Morris, we care comparatively little for the development of the plot. . . . In "Adam Bede" we learn first to know the main actors by their conduct in a number of little scenes, most admirably devised and drawn, and serving to bring out, if not a more powerful, a more elaborate and minute manifestation of their inmost feelings. When we come to the critical parts in the story, and the final catastrophe, they are less interesting and vivid than the preliminary detail of apparently insignificant events. The trial and the arrival of the reprieve are probably the weakest and most commonplace passages; and what we really remember and enjoy are the little scenes on the village green, in Mrs. Poyser's dairy, and Adam Bede's workshop. We have there learnt to know the people themselves, and we scarcely care for what happens to them. The method is natural to a feminine observer who has learnt to interpret character by watching its manifestations in little everyday incidents, and feels comparatively at a loss when having to deal with the more exciting struggles and calamities which make a noise in the world. And therefore, as I think, George Eliot is always more admirable in careful exposition—in setting her personages before us—than in dealing with her catastrophes, where, to say the truth, she sometimes seems to become weak just when we expect her full powers to be exerted.

This is true, for example, of "Silas Marner," where the inimitable opening is very superior to the sequel. It is still more conspicuously true of the "Mill on the Floss." The first part of that novel appears to me to mark the culmination of her genius. So far, it is one of the rare books which it is difficult to praise in adequate language. We may naturally suspect that part of the singular vividness is due to some admixture of an autobiographical element. The sonnets called "Brother and Sister" —perhaps her most successful poetical effort—suggest that the adventures of Tom and Maggie had some counterpart in personal experience. In any case, the whole account of Maggie's childhood, the admirable pathos of the childish yearnings, and the quaint chorus of uncles and aunts, the adventure with the gipsies, the wanderings by the Floss, the visit to Tom in his school, have a freshness and brilliance of colouring showing that the workmanship is as perfect as the sentiment is tender. But when Maggie ceases to be the most fascinating child in fiction, and becomes the heroine of a novel, the falling off is grievous. The unlucky affair with Stephen Guest is simply indefensible. It may, indeed, be urged—and urged with plausibility—that it is true to nature; it is true, that is, that women of genius—and, indeed, other women—do not always show that taste in the selection of lovers which commends itself to the masculine mind. There is nothing contrary to experience in the supposition that the imagination of an impulsive girl may transfigure a very second-rate young tradesman into a lover worthy of her; but this does not excuse the author for sharing the illusion. It is painfully true that some women, otherwise excellent, may be tempted, like Janet Dempster, to take to stimulants. But we should not have been satisfied if her weakness had been represented as a creditable or venial peculiarity, or without a sense of the degradation. So it would, in any case, be hardly pleasant to make our charming Maggie the means of illustrating the doctrine that a woman of high qualities may throw herself away upon a low creature; when she is made to act in this way, and the weakness is not duly emphasised, we are forced to suppose that George Eliot did not see what a poor creature she has really drawn. Perhaps this is characteristic of a certain feminine incapacity for drawing really masculine heroes, which is exemplified, not quite so disagreeably, in the case of Dorothea and Ladislaw. But it is a misfortune, and all the more so because the error seems to be gratuitous. If it was necessary to introduce a new lover, he should have been endowed with some qualities likely to attract Maggie's higher nature, instead of betraying his second-rate dandyism in every feature. But the engagement to Philip Wakem, who is, at least, a lovable character, might surely have supplied enough tragical motive for a catastrophe which would not degrade poor Maggie to common clay. As it is, what promises to be the most perfect story of its kind ends most pathetically indeed, but yet with a strain which jars most painfully upon the general harmony.

The line so sharply drawn in the "Mill on the Floss" is also the boundary between two provinces of the whole region. With Maggie's visit to St. Ogg's, we take leave of that part of George Eliot's work which can be praised without important qualification—of work so admirable in its kind that we have a sense of complete achievement. In the later stories we come upon debatable ground: we have to recognise distinct failure in hitting the mark, and to strike a balance between the good and bad qualities, instead of simply recognising the thorough harmony of a finished whole. What is the nature of the change? The shortcomings are, as I have said, obvious enough. We have, for example, the growing tendency to substitute elaborate analysis for direct presentation; there are such passages, as one to which I have referred, where we are told that it is necessary to understand Deronda's character at five-and-twenty in order to appreciate the effect of after-events; and where we have an elaborate discussion which would be perfectly admissible in the discussion of some historical character, but which, in a writer who has the privilege of creating history, strikes us as an evasion of a difficulty. When we are limited to certain facts, we are forced to theorise as to the qualities which they indicate. Real people do not always get into situations which speak for themselves. But when we can make such facts as will reveal character, we have no right to give the abstract theory for the concrete embodiment. We perceive when this is done that the reflective faculties have been growing at the expense of the imagination, and that, instead of simply enriching and extending the field of interest, they are coming into the foreground and usurping functions for which they are unfitted. The fault is palpable in "Romola." The remarkable power not only of many passages but of the general conception of the book is unable to blind us to the fact that, after all, it is a magnificent piece of cram. The masses of information have not been fused by a glowing imagination. The fuel has put out the fire. If we fail to perceive this in the more serious passages, it is painfully evident in those which are meant to be humorous or playful. People often impose upon themselves when they are listening to some rhetoric, perhaps because, when we have got into a reverential frame of mind, our critical instincts are in abeyance. But it is not so easy to simulate amusement. And if anybody, with the mimicry of Mrs. Poyser or Bob Jakin in his mind, can get through the chapter called "A Florentine Joke" without coming to the conclusion that the jokes of that period were oppressive and wearisome ghosts of the facetious, he must be one of those people who take in jokes by the same faculty as scientific theorems. If we are indulgent, it must be on the ground that the historical novel proper is after all an elaborate blunder. It is really analogous to, and shows the weakness of, the various attempts at the revival of extinct phases of art with which we have been overpowered in these days. It almost inevitably falls into Scylla or Charybdis; it is either a heavy mass of information striving to be lively, or it is really lively at the price of being thoroughly shallow, and giving us the merely pretty and picturesque in place of the really impressive. If anyone has succeeded in avoiding the horns of this dilemma, it is certainly not George Eliot. She had certainly very imposing authorities on her side; but I imagine that "Romola"

gives unqualified satisfaction only to people who hold that academical correctness of design can supply the place of vivid directness of intuitive vision.

Yet the situation was not so much the cause as the symptom of a change. When George Eliot returned to her proper ground, she did not regain the old magic. "Middlemarch" is undoubtedly a powerful book, but to many readers it is a rather painful book, and it can hardly be called a charming book to anyone. The light of common day has most unmistakably superseded the indescribable glow which illuminated the earlier writings.

The change, so far as we need consider it, is sufficiently indicated by one circumstance. The "prelude" invites us to remember Saint Theresa. Her passionate nature, we are told, demanded a consecration of life to some object of unselfish devotion. She found it in the reform of a religious order. But there are many modern Theresas who, with equally noble aspirations, can find no worthy object for their energies. They have found "no coherent social faith and order," no sufficient guidance for their ardent souls. And thus we have now and then a Saint Theresa, "foundress of nothing, whose loving heart-beats and sobs after an unattained goodness tremble off and are dispersed among hindrances instead of centring in some long recognisable deed." This, then, is the keynote of "Middlemarch." We are to have one more variation on the theme already treated in various form; and Dorothea Brooke is to be the Saint Theresa with lofty aspirations to pass through a searching ordeal, and, if she fails in outward results, yet to win additional nobility from failure. And yet, if this be the design, it almost seems as if the book were intended for elaborate irony. Dorothea starts with some admirable, though not very novel, aspirations of the social kind with a desire to improve drainage and provide better cottages for the poor. She meets a consummate pedant, who is piteously ridiculed for his petty and hidebound intellect, and immediately takes him to be her hero and guide to lofty endeavour. She fancies, as we are told, that her spiritual difficulties will be solved by the help of a little Latin and Greek. "Perhaps even Hebrew might be necessary—at least the alphabet and a few roots—in order to arrive at the core of things and judge soundly on the social duties of the Christian." She marries Mr. Casaubon, and of course is speedily undeceived. But, curiously enough, the process of enlightenment seems to be very partial. Her faith in her husband receives its death-blow as soon as she finds out—not that he is a wretched pedant, but that he is a pedant of the wrong kind. Will Ladislaw points out to her that Mr. Casaubon is throwing away his labour because he does not know German, and is therefore only abreast of poor old Jacob Bryant in the last century, instead of being a worthy contemporary of Professor Max Müller. Surely Dorothea's error is almost as deep as ever. Casaubon is a wretched being because he has neither heart nor brains— not because his reading has been confined to the wrong set of books. Surely a man may be a prig and a pedant, though he is familiar with the very last researches of German professors. The latest theories about comparative mythology may be familiar to a man with a soul comparable only to a dry pea in a bladder. If Casaubon had been all that Dorothea fancied, if his knowledge had been thoroughly up to the mark, we should still have pitied her for her not knowing the difference between a man and a stick. Unluckily, she never seems to find out that in this stupendous blunder, and not in the pardonable ignorance as to the true value of his literary labours, is the real source of her misfortune. In fact, she hardly seems to grow wiser even at the end; for when poor Casaubon is as dead as his writings, she takes up with a young gentleman who appears to have some good feeling, but is conspicuously unworthy of the affections of a Saint

Theresa. Had "Middlemarch" been intended for a cutting satire upon the aspirations of young ladies who wish to learn Latin and Greek when they ought to be nursing babies and supporting hospitals, these developments of affairs would have been in perfect congruity with the design. As it is, we are left with the feeling that aspirations of this kind scarcely deserve a better fate than they meet, and that Dorothea was all the better for getting the romantic aspirations out of her head. Have not the commonplace people the best of the argument?

It would be very untrue to say that the later books show any defect of general power. I do not think, for example, that there are many passages in modern fiction so vigorous as the description of poor Lydgate, whose higher aspirations are dashed with a comparatively vulgar desire for worldly success, gradually engulfed by the selfish persistence of his wife, like a swimmer sucked down by an octopus. On the contrary, the picture is so forcible and so lifelike that one reads it with a sense of actual bitterness. And as in "Daniel Deronda," though I am ready to confess that Mordecai and Daniel are to my mind intolerable bores, I hold the story of Grandecourt and Gwendolen to be, though not a pleasant, a singularly powerful study. And it may certainly be said both of "Romola" and of "Middlemarch" that they have some merits of so high an order that the defects upon which I have dwelt are felt as blemishes, not as fatal errors. If there is some misunderstanding of the limits of her own powers, or some misconception of true artistic conditions, nobody can read them without the sense of having been in contact with a comprehensive and vigorous intellect, with high feeling and keen powers of observation. Only one cannot help regretting the loss of that early charm. In reading "Adam Bede," we feel first the magic, and afterwards we recognise the power which it implies. In "Middlemarch" we feel the power, but we ask in vain for the charm. Some such change passes over any great mind which goes through a genuine process of development. It is not surprising that the reflective powers should become more predominant in later years; that reasoning should to some extent take the place of intuitive perception; and that experience of life should give a sterner and sadder tone to the implied criticism of human nature. We are prepared to find less spontaneity, less freshness of interest in the little incidents of life, and we are not surprised that a mind so reflective and richly stored should try to get beyond the charmed circle of its early successes and to give us a picture of wider and less picturesque aspects of human life. But this does not seem to account sufficiently for the presence of something jarring and depressing in the later work.

Without going into the question fully, one thing may be said: the modern Theresa, whether she is called Dorothea, or Maggie, or Dinah, or Janet, is the central figure in the world of George Eliot's imagination. We are to be brought to sympathise with the noble aspirations of a loving and unselfish spirit, conscious that it cannot receive any full satisfaction within the commonplace conditions of this prosaic world. How women are to find a worthier sphere of action than the mere suckling of babes and chronicling of small beer is a question for the Social Science Associations. Some people answer it by proposing to give women votes or degrees, and others would tell us that such problems can only be answered by reverting to Saint Theresa's method. The solution in terms of actual conduct lies beyond the proper province of the novelist. She has done all that she can do if she has revealed the intrinsic beauty of such a character, and its proper function in life. She should make us fall in love with Romola and Maggie, and convert us to the belief that they are the true salt of the earth.

Up to a certain point her success is complete, and it is won by high moral feeling and quick sympathy with true nobility of character. We pay willing homage to these pure and lofty feminine types, and we may get some measure of the success by comparing them with other dissatisfied heroines whose aspirations are by no means so lofty or so compatible with delicate moral sentiment. But the triumph has its limits. In the sweet old-world country life a Janet or a Dinah can find some sort of satisfaction from an evangelical preacher, or within the limits of the Methodist church. If the thoughts and ways of her circle are narrow, it is in harmony with itself, and we may feel its beauty without asking awkward questions. But as soon as Maggie has left her quiet fields and reached even such a centre of civilisation as St. Ogg's, there is a jar and a discord. "Romola" is in presence of a great spiritual disturbance where the highest aspirations are doomed to the saddest failure; and when we get to "Middlemarch" we feel that the charm has somehow vanished. Even in the early period, Mrs. Poyser's bright common-sense has some advantages over Dinah Morris's highwrought sentiment. And in "Middlemarch" we feel more decidedly that high aspirations are doubtful qualifications; that the ambitious young devotee of science has to compound with the quarrelling world, and the brilliant young Dorothea to submit to a decided clipping of her wings. Is it worth while to have a lofty nature in such surroundings? The very bitterness with which the triumph of the lower characters is set forth seems to betray a kind of misgiving. And it is the presence of this feeling, as well as the absence of the old picturesque scenery, that gives a tone of melancholy to the later books. Some readers are disposed to sneer, and to look upon the heroes and heroines as male and female prigs, who are ridiculous if they persist and contemptible when they fail. Others are disposed to infer that the philosophy which they represent is radically unsatisfactory. And some may say that, after all, the picture is true, however sad, and that, in all ages, people

Discussions of George Eliot

who try to lift their heads above the crowd must lay their account with martyrdom and be content to be uncomfortable. The moral, accepted by George Eliot herself, is indicated at the end of "Middlemarch." A new Theresa, she tells us, will not have the old opportunity any more than a new Antigone would "spend heroic piety in daring all for the sake of a brother's funeral; the medium in which these ardent deeds took shape is for ever gone." There will be many Dorotheas, and some of them doomed to worse sacrifices than the Dorothea of "Middlemarch," and we must be content to think that her influence spent itself through many invisible channels, but was not the less potent because unseen.

Perhaps that is not a very satisfactory conclusion. I cannot here ask why it should not have been more satisfactory. We must admit that there is something rather depressing in the thought of these anonymous Dorotheas feeling about vaguely for some worthy outlet of their energies, taking up with a man of science and discovering him to be an effete pedant, wishing ardently to reform the world, but quite unable to specify the steps to be taken, and condescend-

ing to put up with a very commonplace life in a vague hope that somehow or other they will do some good. Undoubtedly we must admit that, wherever the fault lies, our Theresas have some difficulty in fully manifesting their excellence. But with all their faults, we feel that they embody the imperfect influence of a nature so lofty in its sentiment, so wide in its sympathies, and so keen in its perceptions, that we may wait long before it will be adequately replaced. The imperfections belong in great measure to a time of vast revolutions in thought which produce artistic discords as well as philosophic anarchy. Lower minds escape the difficulty because they are lower; and even to be fully sensitive to the deepest searchings of heart of the time is to possess a high claim on our respect. At lowest, however we may differ from George Eliot's teaching on many points, we feel her to be one who, in the midst of great perplexities, has brought great intellectual powers to setting before us a lofty moral ideal, and, in spite of manifest shortcomings, has shown certain aspects of a vanishing social phase with a power and delicacy unsurpassed in her own sphere.

Final judgment is intellectual contribution of

Marcel Proust

Notes on George Eliot

IN *Adam Bede* the thing that strikes me is the careful, detailed, respectful, poetic and sympathetic portrayal of the humblest and most hardworking walk of life. To keep one's kitchen spotlessly clean is a prime duty, almost a religious duty, and a duty that is a pleasure too. Another striking thing is the sense of gravity attached to an evil intention or to a failure of resolution, which because of the interdependence of mankind spreads its fatal repercussions in every direction; and another, the sense of the mysterious greatness of human life and the life of nature, the solemn mysteries in which we play a part while knowing no more about them than does the growing flower (cf. *Silas Marner*). Then there is the sense that above the sequence of our vices and misfortunes a mighty providence somehow sustains a higher order that turns our evil into the incomprehensible instrument of our good (cf. *Silas Marner*). Adam loses Hetty, and this had to be, so that his heart might be opened to love the child (cf. Emerson, *Compensation,* and "man hurries about and God leads him"). Extremely sensitive feeling for nature, entering into it rather than describing it; above all, for nature in tranquillity; sweetness of autumn days, beauty of meadows and woodland, evenings of fast-travelling clouds. An exact, colourful, shrewd, eloquent way of fitting dialogue to humorous characters without lapsing into farce, with a dry wit as in Anatole France. Sense of the changes taking place in us and in things during the course of our lives. Silas's return to [Lantern] Yard, etc. Here and there, proofs of being familiar with philosophy (terms . . . imagery, etc.).

Freshness of imagery, springing from a sensitive, unjaded way of looking at things, that discovers unobserved feelings in them and so can describe them as symbols of feelings that are analogous (hearts thawing like little brooks); rather ponderous jokes about the nobility and gentry.

Sense of the good wrought by suffering, of moral growth, of counterpoising moral reactions through the social scale: here, about a flight of birds, here, about a church-going, elsewhere, about a gambler's losses.

A conservative spirit; not too much book-learning, not too many railways, not too much religious reform.

A genuine feeling for the bent of mind in a carpenter, a weaver, etc.

A lively sense of the development of sympathy and liking between people. . . .

Progressive capitulation of will power; we leave the baby's mother in *Silas* resolved against taking any more opium, and we find her with the bottle emptied. M. . . resolved not to see Hetty again, a moment later in her arms.

Sense that suffering is greater in a person who has no spiritual life, no moral solidarity with others.

One of the conclusions to be drawn from these books (and one that is not pointed out) is that the evil we do *is* evil (we work evil to ourselves and to others). And that on the other hand the evil which befalls us is often the necessary condition of a greater good that God intended for us.

Reprinted from *Marcel Proust on Art and Literature,* © copyright 1958 by Meridian Books, Inc. Translation © Chatto and Windus, Ltd., 1957. Originally published in French by Librairies Gallimard, Paris, 1954, under the title *Contre Sainte-Beuve.* Used by permission of Meridian Books, Inc.

Virginia Woolf

George Eliot

To READ George Eliot attentively is to become aware how little one knows about her. It is also to become aware of the credulity, not very creditable to one's insight, with which, half consciously and partly maliciously, one had accepted the late Victorian version of a deluded woman who held phantom sway over subjects even more deluded than herself. At what moment and by what means her spell was broken it is difficult to ascertain. Some people attribute it to the publication of her *Life*. Perhaps George Meredith, with his phrase about the "mercurial little showman" and the "errant woman" on the daïs, gave point and poison to the arrows of thousands incapable of aiming them so accurately, but delighted to let fly. She became one of the butts for youth to laugh at, the convenient symbol of a group of serious people who were all guilty of the same idolatry and could be dismissed with the same scorn. Lord Acton had said that she was greater than Dante; Herbert Spencer exempted her novels, as if they were not novels, when he banned all fiction from the London Library. She was the pride and paragon of her sex. Moreover, her private record was not more alluring than her public. Asked to describe an afternoon at the Priory, the story-teller always intimated that the memory of those serious Sunday afternoons had come to tickle his sense of humour. He had been so much alarmed by the grave lady in her low chair; he had been so anxious to say the intelligent thing. Certainly, the talk had been very serious, as a note in the fine clear hand of the great novelist bore witness. It was dated on the Monday morning, and she accused herself of having spoken without due forethought of Marivaux when she meant another; but no doubt, she said, her listener had already supplied the correction. Still, the memory of talking about Marivaux to George Eliot on a Sunday afternoon was not a romantic memory. It had faded with the passage of the years. It had not become picturesque. . . .

The books which followed so soon after her union testify in the fullest manner to the great liberation which had come to her with personal happiness. In themselves they provide us with a plentiful feast. Yet at the threshold of her literary career one may find in some of the circumstances of her life influences that turned her mind to the past, to the country village, to the quiet and beauty and simplicity of childish memories and away from herself and the present. We understand how it was that her first book was *Scenes of Clerical Life*, and not *Middlemarch*. Her union with Lewes had surrounded her with affection, but in view of the circumstances and of the conventions it had also isolated her. "I wish it to be understood," she wrote in 1857, "that I should never invite any one to come and see me who did not ask for the invitation." She had been "cut off from what is called the world," she said later, but she did not regret it. By becoming thus marked, first by circumstances and later, inevitably, by her fame, she lost the power to move on equal terms unnoted among her kind; and the loss for a novelist was

From *The Common Reader* by Virginia Woolf, copyright, 1925, by Harcourt, Brace and Company, Inc.; renewed, 1953, by Leonard Woolf. Reprinted by permission of Harcourt, Brace and Company, Inc.

Virginia Woolf

serious. Still, basking in the light and sunshine of *Scenes of Clerical Life,* feeling the large mature mind spreading itself with a luxurious sense of freedom in the world of her "remotest past," to speak of loss seems inappropriate. Everything to such a mind was gain. All experience filtered down through layer after layer of perception and reflection, enriching and nourishing. The utmost we can say, in qualifying her attitude towards fiction by what little we know of her life, is that she had taken to heart certain lessons not usually learnt early, if learnt at all, among which, perhaps, the most branded upon her was the melancholy virtue of tolerance; her sympathies are with the everyday lot, and play most happily in dwelling upon the homespun of ordinary joys and sorrows. She has none of that romantic intensity which is connected with a sense of one's own individuality, unsated and unsubdued, cutting its shape sharply upon the background of the world. What were the loves and sorrows of a snuffy old clergyman, dreaming over his whisky, to the fiery egotism of Jane Eyre? The beauty of those first books, *Scenes of Clerical Life, Adam Bede, The Mill on the Floss,* is very great. It is impossible to estimate the merit of the Poysers, the Dodsons, the Gilfils, the Bartons, and the rest with all their surroundings and dependencies, because they have put on flesh and blood and we move among them, now bored, now sympathetic, but always with that unquestioning acceptance of all that they say and do, which we accord to the great originals only. The flood of memory and humour which she pours so spontaneously into one figure, one scene after another, until the whole fabric of ancient rural England is revived, has so much in common with a natural process that it leaves us with little consciousness that there is anything to criticise. We accept; we feel the delicious warmth and release of spirit which the great creative writers alone procure for us. As one comes back to the books after years

of absence they pour out, even against our expectation, the same store of energy and heat, so that we want more than anything to idle in the warmth as in the sun beating down from the red orchard wall. If there is an element of unthinking abandonment in thus submitting to the humours of Midland farmers and their wives, that, too, is right in the circumstances. We scarcely wish to analyse what we feel to be so large and deeply human. And when we consider how distant in time the world of Shepperton and Hayslope is, and how remote the minds of farmer and agricultural labourers from those of most of George Eliot's readers, we can only attribute the ease and pleasure with which we ramble from house to smithy, from cottage parlour to rectory garden, to the fact that George Eliot makes us share their lives, not in a spirit of condescension or of curiosity, but in a spirit of sympathy. She is no satirist. The movement of her mind was too slow and cumbersome to lend itself to comedy. But she gathers in her large grasp a great bunch of the main elements of human nature and groups them loosely together with a tolerant and wholesome understanding which, as one finds upon re-reading, has not only kept her figures fresh and free, but has given them an unexpected hold upon our laughter and tears. There is the famous Mrs. Poyser. It would have been easy to work her idiosyncrasies to death, and, as it is, perhaps, George Eliot gets her laugh in the same place a little too often. But memory, after the book is shut, brings out, as sometimes in real life, the details and subtleties which some more salient characteristic has prevented us from noticing at the time. We recollect that her health was not good. There were occasions upon which she said nothing at all. She was patience itself with a sick child. She doted upon Totty. Thus one can muse and speculate about the greater number of George Eliot's characters and find, even in the least important, a roominess and margin where those qualities lurk which she has no call to bring from their obscurity.

But in the midst of all this tolerance and sympathy there are, even in the early books, moments of greater stress. Her humour has shown itself broad enough to cover a wide range of fools and failures, mothers and children, dogs and flourishing midland fields, farmers, sagacious or fuddled over their ale, horse-dealers, inn-keepers, curates, and carpenters. Over them all broods a certain romance, the only romance that George Eliot allowed herself—the romance of the past. The books are astonishingly readable and have no trace of pomposity or pretence. But to the reader who holds a large stretch of her early work in view it will become obvious that the mist of recollection gradually withdraws. It is not that her power diminishes, for, to our thinking, it is at its highest in the mature *Middlemarch*, the magnificent book which with all its imperfections is one of the few English novels written for grown-up people. But the world of fields and farms no longer contents her. In real life she had sought her fortunes elsewhere; and though to look back into the past was calming and consoling, there are, even in the early works, traces of that troubled spirit, that exacting and questioning and baffled presence who was George Eliot herself. In *Adam Bede* there is a hint of her in Dinah. She shows herself far more openly and completely in Maggie in *The Mill on the Floss*. She is Janet in *Janet's Repentance*, and Romola, and Dorothea seeking wisdom and finding one scarcely knows what in marriage with Ladislaw. Those who fall foul of George Eliot do so, we incline to think, on account of her heroines; and with good reason; for there is no doubt that they bring out the worst of her, lead her into difficult places, make her self-conscious, didactic, and occasionally vulgar. Yet if you could delete the whole sisterhood you would leave a much smaller and a much inferior world, albeit a world of greater artistic perfection and far superior jollity

and comfort. In accounting for her failure, in so far as it was a failure, one recollects that she never wrote a story until she was thirty-seven, and that by the time she was thirty-seven she had come to think of herself with a mixture of pain and something like resentment. For long she preferred not to think of herself at all. Then, when the first flush of creative energy was exhausted and self-confidence had come to her, she wrote more and more from the personal standpoint, but she did so without the unhesitating abandonment of the young. Her self-consciousness is always marked when her heroines say what she herself would have said. She disguised them in every possible way. She granted them beauty and wealth into the bargain; she invented, more improbably, a taste for brandy. But the disconcerting and stimulating fact remained that she was compelled by the very power of her genius to step forth in person upon the quiet bucolic scene.

The noble and beautiful girl who insisted upon being born into the Mill on the Floss is the most obvious example of the ruin which a heroine can strew about her. Humour controls her and keeps her lovable so long as she is small and can be satisfied by eloping with the gipsies or hammering nails into her doll; but she develops; and before George Eliot knows what has happened she has a full-grown woman on her hands demanding what neither gipsies, nor dolls, nor St. Ogg's itself is capable of giving her. First Philip Wakem is produced, and later Stephen Guest. The weakness of the one and the coarseness of the other have often been pointed out; but both, in their weaknes and coarseness, illustrate not so much George Eliot's inability to draw the portrait of a man, as the uncertainty, the infirmity, and the fumbling which shook her hand when she had to conceive a fit mate for a heroine. She is in the first place driven beyond the home world she knew and loved, and forced to set foot in middle-class drawing-rooms where young men sing all the summer morning and young women sit embroidering smoking-caps for bazaars. She feels herself out of her element, as her clumsy satire of what she calls "good society" proves.

Good society has its claret and its velvet carpets, its dinner engagements six weeks deep, its opera, and its faëry ball rooms . . . gets its science done by Faraday and its religion by the superior clergy who are to be met in the best houses; how should it have need of belief and emphasis?

There is no trace of humour or insight there, but only the vindictiveness of a grudge which we feel to be personal in its origin. But terrible as the complexity of our social system is in its demands upon the sympathy and discernment of a novelist straying across the boundaries, Maggie Tulliver did worse than drag George Eliot from her natural surroundings. She insisted upon the introduction of the great emotional scene. She must love; she must despair; she must be drowned clasping her brother in her arms. The more one examines the great emotional scenes the more nervously one anticipates the brewing and gathering and thickening of the cloud which will burst upon our heads at the moment of crisis in a shower of disillusionment and verbosity. It is partly that her hold upon dialogue, when it is not dialect, is slack; and partly that she seems to shrink with an elderly dread of fatigue from the effort of emotional concentration. She allows her heroines to talk too much. She has little verbal felicity. She lacks the unerring taste which chooses one sentence and compresses the heart of the scene within that. "Whom are you going to dance with?" asked Mr. Knightley, at the Westons' ball. "With you, if you will ask me," said Emma; and she has said enough. Mrs. Casaubon would have talked for an hour and we should have looked out of the window. Yet, dismiss the heroines without sympathy, confine George Eliot to the agricultural

world of her "remotest past," and you not only diminish her greatness but lose her true flavour. That greatness is here we can have no doubt. The width of the prospect, the large strong outlines of the principal features, the ruddy light of the early books, the searching power and reflective richness of the later tempt us to linger and expatiate beyond our limits. But it is upon the heroines that we would cast a final glance. "I have always been finding out my religion since I was a little girl," says Dorothea Casaubon. "I used to pray so much—now I hardly ever pray. I try not to have desires merely for myself. . . ." She is speaking for them all. That is their problem. They cannot live without religion, and they start out on the search for one when they are little girls. Each has the deep feminine passion for goodness, which makes the place where she stands in aspiration and agony the heart of the book—still and cloistered like a place of worship, but that she no longer knows to whom to pray. In learning they seek their goal; in the ordinary tasks of womanhood; in the wider service of their kind. They do not find what they seek, and we cannot wonder. The ancient consciousness of woman, charged with suffering and sensibility, and for so many ages dumb, seems in them to have brimmed and overflowed and uttered a demand for something —they scarcely know what—for something that is perhaps incompatible with the facts of human existence. George Eliot had far too strong an intelligence to tamper with those facts, and too broad a humour to mitigate the truth because it was a stern one. Save for the supreme courage of their endeavour, the struggle ends, for her heroines, in tragedy, or in a compromise that is even more melancholy. But their story is the incomplete version of the story of George Eliot herself. For her, too, the burden and the complexity of womanhood were not enough; she must reach beyond the sanctuary and pluck for herself the strange bright fruits of art and knowledge.

Clasping them as few women have ever clasped them, she would not renounce her own inheritance—the difference of view, the difference of standard—nor accept an inappropriate reward. Thus we behold her, a memorable figure, inordinately praised and shrinking from her fame, despondent, reserved, shuddering back into the arms of love as if there alone were satisfaction and, it might be, justification, at the same time reaching out with "a fastidious yet hungry ambition" for all that life could offer the free and inquiring mind and confronting her feminine aspirations with the real world of men. Triumphant was the issue for her, whatever it may have been for her creations, and as we recollect all that she dared and achieved, how with every obstacle against her—sex and health and convention—she sought more knowledge and more freedom till the body, weighted with its double burden, sank worn out, we must lay upon her grave whatever we have it in our power to bestow of laurel and rose.

Lord David Cecil

George Eliot

. . . George Eliot's serious characters, then, are envisaged exclusively in their moral aspect. They are portraits of the inner man, but portraits not designed like Charlotte Brontë's to exhibit the colour of his temperament, but the principles of his conduct—his besetting sin, his presiding virtue. Such a portrait inevitably omits many of those aspects of a man—his manner, his mood, his face—which make living most of the great figures of fiction. All the same, George Eliot's concentration on the moral side of human nature is the chief source of her peculiar glory, the kernel of her precious unique contribution to our literature. Her imagination is not a distorting glass like Dickens', vitalising her figures by accentuating their personal idiosyncrasies, nor is it, like Charlotte Brontë's, a painted window suffusing them with the colour of her own live temperament; it is an X-ray, bringing them to life by the clearness with which she penetrates to the secret mainspring of their actions.

Once more it is her intellect which is the source of her success. Her power of drawing conclusions gave her a naturally sharp eye for symptoms of moral strength and weakness, taught her to discern them in all their varying modes of expression in well brought up girls, in men of the world, a poor weaver, a lusty young man, to note that Dr Lydgate did not take trouble with an ugly woman, that Hetty Sorrel always avoided being left to look after the children. She could also distinguish between different varieties of the same characteristic; see how Dorothea's sense of duty differed from Mary Garth's, Godfrey Cass's self-indulgence from that of Arthur Donnithorne. And she took advantage of her observation. She traced these expressions of virtue and weakness to their original source in the character, discovered the spark of nobility, the streak of weakness which are their origin. Finally her disciplined generalising intelligence taught her to see the significance of her discoveries. Having analysed a character into its elements, she was able to distinguish their relative force and position. She could deduce its central principle so that, however complex and inconsistent it might appear, she saw it as a unity. It is this grasp of psychological essentials which gives her characters their reality. We may not *see* Godfrey Cass as we *see* Pickwick, but we understand him. We get behind the clock face and see the works, locate the mainspring, discover how it makes the wheels turn. We know just how he will behave and why; we know exactly what special mixture of common human ingredients makes him act differently from other people.

This clear-sighted vision of the essentials of character gives George Eliot certain advantages over the other Victorians. For one thing it means that her characters, unlike theirs, are always consistent. Dickens and Charlotte Brontë, as we have seen, intent on the outward man, often fail to make the inner consistent; Mr Micawber suddenly and incredibly turns into an efficient mayor, the conventional Mrs Reed commits a criminal act. Trollope's characters, it is true, never act with outrageous inconsistency, his sense of probability is too great for that. But they do not always act

From *Early Victorian Novelists* by Lord David Cecil, copyright © 1935, used by special permission of the publishers, The Bobbs-Merrill Company, Inc.

inevitably. But George Eliot's characters act inevitably, under the irresistible force of their directing principle: so that they are always true to themselves. Through every change of fortune, every variety of circumstance, they remain the same clear recognisable individual moral entities.

But it is not only in this consistency that George Eliot's intellectual understanding of her characters gives her an advantage over the other Victorians. It also enables her to describe aspects of human nature which they cannot. It gives her the power which won her the admiration of Proust, the power to describe successfully how a character develops. This is very rare among novelists. When they want to describe a good man going to the bad, for instance, they generally cut him into two; we are shown a good man in the first part of the book, and a bad man in the second. But they do not seem the same man. We have seen nothing in the first to lead us to understand how he becomes the second. In their efforts to show the change that overtook him, they forget to maintain those constant characteristics which keep him one person. Not so George Eliot. For her perception of these characteristics is the root of her whole conception. Lydgate, on his first appearance in *Middlemarch,* is an enthusiastic and disinterested young doctor, only intent on extending the boundaries of knowledge and with a scorn for the worldly prizes that his profession might enable him to gain. At the end he is a fashionable physician with no interest in discovery, content only to maintain a prosperous practice. George Eliot portrays the evidences of this change with extraordinary acuteness of observation. We see how it has lowered his spirits, slackened his scruples, embittered his tongue. But for all that he is so altered, we recognise him as the same Lydgate as we saw at first; nor do we find the change inexplicable. For, from his entry on the scene, we have been made aware of the weak spot in Lydgate's character, his dislike of doing something

disagreeable to himself, and we can see that in difficult circumstances this weakness will render impotent his strongest ambitions. Moreover, George Eliot knows just how to show how this is most likely to have happened. The situations in which she has involved Lydgate are precisely those most likely to find out his weakness: and she can exhibit exactly the mode by which, step by step, he gives way to it, readjusts his principles to suit his practice, till imperceptibly he is transformed to the man of his final phase.

In a similar way we see Silas Marner grow from an enthusiastic austere Methodist, careless of this world's goods, first into a miser, dominated by desire to increase his store of gold, and then, under the influence of the child Eppie, change a second time to a generous, affectionate old man with no thought but the good of others. These changes are not surprising to us, for from the first we have been made to realise that Marner is one of those nervous diffident characters, whose whole life is directed by the necessity of finding some outside object on which they can depend for support. The religious community in which he is brought up is his first prop; when this fails him he inevitably retires into terrified solitude; and in solitude inevitably turns to the only solid good left on his horizon, the money he makes. Finally, when this money is stolen and an orphan child deposited at his door, we see it as equally inevitable that he should devote himself completely to the child—and that such a devotion should bring out his latent good qualities. In all vicissitudes he is demonstrably the same character.

Again, George Eliot's grip on psychological essentials enables her to draw complex characters better than her predecessors. Novelists who draw from outside like Trollope have no difficulty in making a simple character convincing; for the reader has only to see its outside clearly to be able to deduce its elements for himself. But when they come to a complex character they fail; for the outer manifestations of such a character are so inconsistent, that unless the reader is given some key to them he simply does not feel that they are expressions of the same person. He cannot understand what sort of woman Lady Ongar is, when her actions seem to contradict each other so sharply. George Eliot's peculiar power makes her able to surmount this difficulty. Drawing from the inside out, starting with the central principle of the character, she is able to show how it reveals itself in the most apparently inconsistent manifestations, can give to the most vari-coloured surface of character that prevalent tone which marks it as the expression of one personality. Her characters always hang together, are of a piece, their defects are the defects of their virtues. We are not surprised that a man so anxious for the good opinion of others as Arthur Donnithorne should selfishly seduce Hetty, because we realise that the controlling force in his character is the desire for immediate enjoyment; so that his wish to sun himself in the pleasant warmth of other people's liking goes along with his inability not to yield to the immediate pleasure of Hetty's embraces. George Eliot can follow the windings of motive through the most tortuous labyrinths, for firmly grasped in her hand is always the central clue. . . .

She is particularly good at showing how temptation triumphs. No other English novelist has given us so vivid a picture of the process of moral defeat, the gradual steps by which Mr Bulstrode is brought to further Raffles' death, Arthur Donnithorne's gradual yielding to his passion for Hetty, Maggie Tulliver's to hers for Stephen Guest. With an inexorable clearness she reveals how temptation insinuates itself into the mind, how it retreats at the first suspicious movement of conscience, how it comes back disguised, and how, if once more vanquished, it will sham death only to arise suddenly and sweep its victim away on a single irresistible gust of desire when he is off his guard. With an extraordinary subtlety she describes Arthur Donnithorne's yielding to his desire to meet Hetty once more: how he conceals his true object even from himself by pretending that he does it only to say farewell, persuades himself that he will be committing an act of gratuitous cruelty if he refuses to see Hetty; or how Maggie's passion for Stephen steals into her inexperienced mind, imperceptibly, so that she only realises it when it has become such an obsession that she is unable to see it in its true proportions. Alone in her room she can make the strongest resolutions, but when Stephen appears the violence of her desire so overwhelms her that she cannot see her conduct in perspective at all. She lives only in the present, and in the present she is only conscious that she is happy and must at all costs prolong her happiness. With equal insight George Eliot can portray the moral chaos that takes possession of the mind after wrong has been done. She exposes all the complex writhings of a spirit striving to make itself at ease on the bed of a disturbed conscience, the desperate casuistry by which it attempts to justify itself, its inexhaustible ingenuity in blinding itself to unpleasant facts, the baseless hopes it conjures up for its comfort; she can distinguish precisely how different an act looks before it is done, shrouded in the softening darkness of the secret heart, and after, exposed in all its naked ugliness to the harsh daylight of other people's judgment. . . .

It is in the treatment of character that George Eliot's more active intellect gives her her most conspicuous advantage over the typical Victorians. But in two other respects her work is a pleasant contrast to theirs. Her level of merit is far more consistently maintained. They, writing as they do from the voluntary impulse of an instinctive imagination, only write well as long as that imagination happens to be working. When their story takes them away from the characters and scenes which inspire them, they write extremely badly. But

George Eliot's inspiration, immanent as it is in the general conception of her book, never wholly ceases to function. Even if the plot involves her in some aspect of life not peculiarly appropriate to her talents, she does not make a complete failure of it. We feel the conception to be good though the execution may be faulty. With her greater consistency goes a greater command of form. Dickens' form or Charlotte Brontë's is imperfect because it is no part of their inspiration, it is a mere makeshift framework to hold their inspiration together; and as often as not it holds it together very badly. Inessential characters and scenes bulge over its edges, deforming its symmetry, concealing its intention. But George Eliot's structure is the very substance of her primary conception. She begins with her situation, her characters and scenes are developed from it. Each has its part to play in her general purpose and none is permitted to play more than this part. No minor character swells to gigantic proportions in George Eliot's novels, dwarfing the principals; her most memorable scenes are always turning points in the action. All is co-ordinated, all is in proportion, all is tidy. For her books are as better organised than Charlotte Brontë's, as the material of which they are composed is larger. Yet she is not admired so much as Charlotte Brontë; she is not even admired so much as Trollope. In spite of the variety of her talents and the width of her scope, in spite of the fact that she is the only novelist of her time who writes on the scale of the great continental novelists, the only novelist who holds the same conception of her art which is held today, her reputation has sustained a more catastrophic slump than that of any of her contemporaries. It is not just that she is not read, that her books stand on the shelves unopened. If people do read her they do not enjoy her. It certainly is odd. All the same it is explicable. The temper of our time has something to do with it. For though she is nearer to us in form and subject than the other Victorians, in point of view she is quite as distant. Indeed, we find her point of view even more alien. This is natural enough. An exclusively moral point of view is, at any time, a bleak and unsatisfying affair. Life is altogether too complex and masterful and mysterious to be ordered into tidy little compartments of right and wrong; and any attempt so to order it inevitably leaves a good deal outside that is both interesting and delightful. Moreover, George Eliot's compartments are conspicuously inadequate ones. The virtues of her admiration, industry, self-restraint, conscientiousness, are drab, negative sort of virtues, they are school teachers' virtues. George Eliot does confront human nature a little like a school teacher; kindly but just, calm but censorious, with birchrod in hand to use as she thinks right, and lists of good and bad conduct marks pinned neatly to her desk. And when we see all the vivid disorderly vitality of human nature ranged before her for carefully measured approval or condemnation, we tend to feel rebellious and resentful.

Nor does she, like some Puritan writers, like Bunyan for instance, sweep away our antipathy to her moral system by the enthusiastic conviction with which she expounds it. It was impossible that she should; she did not feel enthusiastic about it herself. Victorian ethical rationalism is the least inspiriting of creeds. For it makes the worst of both worlds: in preserving the moral half of Puritanism, it keeps all that makes it depressing; in rejecting its religious half, it abandons all that gives it zest. Bunyan could preach the ascetic life with enthusiasm, because he felt it would be rewarded by an eternity of ineffable bliss; for him the strait and narrow way was transfigured by the glory which shone from its celestial goal. Moreover, his imagination, deprived though it might be of sensual stimulus, can solace itself with gods and angels and demons, with the wild flames of hell and the starry flowers of paradise. George Eliot's imagination had to scrape what nourishment it could from the bare bones of Puritan ethics; her narrow way led beneath a dull sky into darkness; she had to persuade herself that a life of self-denial was sufficiently rewarded by the consciousness of virtue. In theory she managed to do this satisfactorily enough; but she was too clear-sighted and too honest not to find it difficult to feel a lively conviction of it, in practice. Even in the stories of her ardent youth, she does not paint the satisfactions of a good conscience in very glowing colours. And when in *Middlemarch* she turned to survey the spectacle of human life in the harsh disillusioning light of mature experience, she clearly found it all she could do to believe that a good conscience was much satisfaction at all. She would not admit this. Desperately she reiterates the articles of her creed, anxiously tries to convince us that Dorothea's unselfish devotion to husband and children made up for her failure to realise her youthful dreams. But she does not even convince herself. Do what she will, she cannot disguise the fact that the thought of Dorothea's life leaves her disappointed, disheartened and depressed. And she communicates her depression to her readers.

Still, George Eliot's point of view should not put us off her books. To let it do so indeed is to fall into her error, to judge things by too exclusively moral a standard. A book is not good in proportion as its moral standard is a right one. Good books have been written from widely different moral standards: and a man of taste should be equally able to enjoy them all. Only he will not be able to do so without a little self-discipline on his part; for though its moral point of view may not determine the merit of a book, it does give it perspective; and if we are to see it in that focus in which its artistic qualities are fully apparent, we must train ourselves to acquiesce for the time being in its moral system, however uncongenial we may find it personally. The optimist must forget his dislike of pessimism while he reads Swift, the ascetic his dislike of sensuality while he reads Gautier, the enlightened person of today must forget his dislike of Puritanism while he reads George Eliot. If he has not the self-command to do this, and does not enjoy her in consequence, he has only himself to blame.

All the same George Eliot's loss of reputation is not wholly undeserved. Even if we do strain ourselves to acquiesce in her point of view, we do not feel her the supreme novelist that her contemporaries did. Her books never give us that intense unalloyed pleasure we get from the greatest masters. Though like Tolstoy she is an interesting critic of life, though she constructs well like Jane Austen, though like Dickens she creates a world, yet when we set her achievement in any of these lines beside those of these famous competitors, we feel something lacking. Somehow we are dissatisfied.

It is easy to see why she fails to stand a comparison with Tolstoy. Her vision of life is smaller. She knows about life in provincial nineteenth-century England, life in Middlemarch, the life of merchants and doctors and squires and humble clergymen and small town politicians: she does not know about the savage or sophisticated, about artists and adventurers and the world of fashion and affairs. Even in *Middlemarch*, there are certain things she does not see. Her assiduously intellectual view made her oblivious of the irrational instinctive aspects of human nature. She can enter into its deliberate purposes and its conscientious scruples, but not into its caprices, its passions, its mysticism. Dinah Morris' moral character is brought vividly before us, but not the quality of the religious ecstasy which inspired it. The conflict between Arthur Donnithorne's conscience and his love is traced with the clearest perception, but we have to take the flavour and fire of that love for granted; George Eliot does not tell us about it. Moreover, like all Victorian rationalists, she is a Philistine. She pays lip-service to art, but like Dorothea Brooke confronted with the statues of the Vatican, she does not really see why people set such a value on it. Constructed within so confined an area of vision, it is inevitable that her criticism of life is inadequate. Compared to Tolstoy's it seems petty, drab, provincial. *Middlemarch* may be the nearest English equivalent to *War and Peace,* but it is a provincial sort of *War and Peace.*

It is also easy to see why her form does not satisfy us as Jane Austen's does. Life is chaotic, art is orderly. The novelist's problem is to evolve an orderly composition which is also a convincing picture of life. It is Jane Austen's triumph that she solves this problem perfectly, fully satisfies the rival claims of life and art. Now George Eliot does not. She sacrifices life to art. Her plots seem too neat and symmetrical to be true. We do not feel them to have grown naturally from their situation like a flower, but to have been put together deliberately and calculatedly like a building. For, in spite of her determination that her story should develop logically, she has not that highest formal faculty which makes development appear inevitable, she has to twist facts to make them fit her purpose. For instance, it is an essential part of her design that Godfrey Cass's marriage should not turn out perfectly happily. For it was only made possible by an act of moral weakness on his part: and her object is to show that such acts always bring their punishment. It should have been quite easy for her to make this seem inevitable. This same weakness that inspired Godfrey's act might have alienated his wife; or his mind might have been poisoned by remorse. But George Eliot vindicates the moral law by making him childless. This is not in the least an inevitable consequence of his act. There is no inherent reason in the nature of things why a morally-feeble man should not beget twenty children. In consequence we feel Godfrey's discontent to be no inevitable expression of the moral law, but a gratuitous piece of poetic justice imposed on him

by the arbitrary will of his creator. Again, the marriage between Dinah and Adam, which provides the happy ending for *Adam Bede,* does not strike us as inevitable; indeed what we have learnt of Adam's taste in women leads us to think it very unlikely. But the moral purpose which directs the story demands that Adam and Dinah, the two virtuous characters in the book, should be adequately rewarded for their virtue. And marrying them to each other seems the handiest reward in the circumstances. In order to achieve structural symmetry George Eliot has been forced to relax her vigilant grip on truth.

However, she might have constructed badly and criticised life inadequately and yet have been as satisfying an author as Dickens. He constructed much worse, and only offered us the most rudimentary criticism of life. Yet she is not as satisfying as he is. For she is as inferior to him in his distinguishing quality as she is to Tolstoy and Jane Austen in theirs: she is inferior to him in creative imaginaton. She had one, as we have seen. But, like Trollope's, it was a relatively mild imagination: it does not unite with its subject to generate the highest intensity of aesthetic life. So that when its creations are set beside those of a white-hot imagination like Dickens', they look pale and lifeless. Her settings, for instance, are as substantial as his and as individual. No other English novelist has revealed the English countryside in the light of its past. But her imagination is not powerful enough to make this light a very vivid one. Compared with Dickens' London, George Eliot's Warwickshire shows a little devitalised: not a first-hand painting but a careful coloured engraving.

Her characters, again, are more variously conceived than his, more consistently constructed and observed more accurately. Lydgate is far more like a real man than Mr Micawber: we know much more about him; he never acts, as Mr Micawber does, out of character. But—he is not so alive. Beside Micawber he looks wooden, static, inanimate. For no aspect of his nature, not even that moral aspect where George Eliot's genius shows itself at its most concentrated, is informed by the highest creative vitality. Or, compare Dorothea Brooke with Elena in Turgenev's *On the Eve*. It is an illuminating comparison. For, national differences apart, they are almost the same character: each is a young girl, noble, romantic, passionate, austere, intolerant of triviality and frivolity, possessed by the desire to sacrifice herself to some altruistic ideal. George Eliot stands the comparison much better than might be expected. Dorothea is as substantial and convincing a character as Elena. Her every side is as clearly apprehended. But she is not so individual, she lacks Elena's unmistakable personal flavour; for, though George Eliot has assembled the elements of her character, she has not been able to fire them with that Promethean spark which fuses them together in the substance of a single personality. It is significant that the inhabitants of George Eliot's world, with the exception of her comic characters, are most real to us when they are not talking. George Eliot's analysis of Maggie Tulliver and Dorothea clearly defines the difference between them. But separate two passages of their conversation from their context, and who shall tell which is speaking? And though in analysis they are individual, even there they are not alive in the intensest sense. They are bodies laid out in the dissecting-room, not moving flesh-and-blood human beings. They never seem, as the greatest figures in fiction do, to have got free from their creators, and to be acting and speaking of their own volition. Behind the puppets we always see the shadow of the puppet master manipulating the strings.

Indeed—and here we come to the root cause of her failure to attain that supreme rank to which she aspired—there was something second-rate in the essential quality of George Eliot's inspiration. Her genius was built on the same grand scale as that of the greatest novelists; but it was not, as theirs was, compounded of the best material. She had more talents than most writers; but they were none of them of the finest calibre. So that though she seeks success in so many fields—and never wholly fails to find it—in none, even at her best, does she reach the level of the masterpieces in that particular kind.

Still, this is not enough to account for the peculiar feeling of dissatisfaction that her books give us. Trollope had a second-rate talent, and, within his limitations, he is perfectly satisfying. No, George Eliot is dissatisfying because, paradoxically, on one side she was much more gifted than Trollope; because she had so much more intellectual force. Her second-rate talents were strong enough to achieve success in a second-rate kind. But her intellect was always forcing her to attempt things that needed supreme talents for their achievement. We are always being brought up with a jerk against her limitations. Her imagination was quite wide enough to cover the ground explored by a domestic novel like *Doctor Thorne*. But it was not wide enough to cover the ground needed for an adequate criticism of life. And her intellect spurred her to attempt such criticism. Again, her sense of form was quite strong enough to have achieved success on the lines of an ordinary conventional plot. It was not strong enough to carry through an action only conditioned by the logical development of the situation. And her intellect inspired her to try such an action. Finally, her intellect tended to reduce such imaginative vitality as she had. For all that Trollope's imagination was as weak as hers, he does now and again achieve a greater intensity of creative life, because he lets it have its head. George Eliot could not let her imagination have its head. Her intellect was always at its side, tugging at the reins, diverting it from its course, weighing it down with a great load of analytic comment.

Yet we cannot regret her intellect. For it is the source of her most original characters and her most memorable passages. In it is engendered that penetration into the moral nature of man, which is her peculiar contribution to our literature. No, the truth is that there was a congenital disproportion in the original composition of George Eliot's talent. It had two sides, intellectual and imaginative. And they were inextricably connected. The intellect was the engine which started the machinery of the imagination working. But the engine was too powerful for the machine: it kept it at a strain at which it could not run smoothly and easily. So that it never produced a wholly satisfactory work of art.

All the same, her achievement is a considerable one, more considerable than that of many more accomplished writers. *Middlemarch* may never give us the same feeling of unalloyed pleasure as *Wives and Daughters* does, but rouses far deeper emotions, sets the mind far more seriously astir. For though she was not a supreme artist, George Eliot was not a minor one; laboriously but surely her insight, her integrity, her sad, mature wisdom, lifted her to the region of major art. When all is said and done she is a great writer; no unworthy heir of Thackeray and Dickens, no unworthy forerunner of Hardy and Henry James. She stands at the gateway between the old novel and the new, a massive caryatid, heavy of countenance, uneasy of attitude; but noble, monumental, profoundly impressive.

S. L. Bethell

The Novels of George Eliot

1

AN EXAMINATION of the opening paragraph of the *Scenes of Clerical Life* may indicate the birth of a new literary genius, but it certainly illustrates also the besetting sins of the age:

"Shepperton Church was a very different-looking building five-and-twenty years ago. To be sure, its substantial stone tower looks at you through its intelligent eye, the clock, with the friendly expression of former days; but in everything else what changes! Now there is a wide span of slate roof flanking the old steeple; the windows are tall and symmetrical; the outer doors are resplendent with oak-graining, the inner doors reverentially noiseless with a garment of red baize; and the walls, you are convinced, no lichen will ever again effect a settlement on—they are smooth and innutrient as the summit of the Rev. Amos Barton's head, after ten years of baldness and supererogatory soap. Pass through the baize doors and you will see the nave filled with well-shaped benches, understood to be free seats; while in certain eligible corners, less directly under the fire of the clergyman's eye, there are pews reserved for the Shepperton gentility. Ample galleries are supported on iron pillars, and in one of them stands the crowning glory, the very clasp or aigrette of Shepperton church-adornment—namely, an organ, not very much out of repair, on which a collector of small rents, differentiated by the force of circumstances into an organist, will accompany the alacrity of your departure after the blessing, by a sacred minuet or an easy 'Gloria.'"

The only point hitherto commented on is the word "innutrient," which seemed to contemporaries unnecessarily scientific. The use of scientific metaphor is a characteristic of George Eliot, and an important one, since it applies a dominant tendency of her period. George Eliot was associated with Herbert Spencer, George Henry Lewes, and other "scientific philosophers," and their influence upon her was great. Counterbalancing this was a conservative tendency due to her early acquaintance with rural life in the Midlands. In *Amos Barton* the conflict is already apparent in the alternating condescension and tenderness of her attitude towards her subject; and since it is a conflict fundamental to her age, recognition of it helps to determine her possible importance, from the outset. But in the *Scenes of Clerical Life* her originality and insight are still obscured by conventional forms of expression, corresponding to conventional modes of feeling and thought. The self-conscious rhythm, the inversion ("in everything else what changes!"), the "friendly expression" of the clock, "former days"; build up an impression of sentimentality, a too Lamblike tenderness for the past. "Intelligent eye," "garment of red baize," are strong indications of an endeavour to be literary; the "supererogatory soap" is the sort of whimsy with a touch of pathos, which the Victorians preferred to satire; and "the crowning glory—the very clasp or aigrette of Shepperton church-adornment," would have delighted the ear (handsome volute to the human capital") of Lamb himself. There is a tendency to use big words because they're funny (*vide* also the "long-eared pachyderms" in Chapter IV); and "sacred minuet" and "easy 'Gloria'" have no intellectual justification for their apparent balance.

On the whole the *Scenes of Clerical Life* betray themselves for what they are; an attempt to write fiction, to do the same sort of thing that others were doing at the same time. The "tone," as Dr. Richards calls the attitude of a writer towards his readers, is somewhere between the posturing of Dickens and the unpleasant condescension of Thackeray (to both which one so much prefers the "honest craftsman" attitude of Wilkie Collins): it bespeaks an endeavour to instruct and amuse. The writer is officiously obtrusive: this is one way of "distancing" the story and relating it to wider issues, but all depends on the manner in which the reader is addressed; there is an example in *Amos Barton*, near the beginning of Chapter V:

"But, my dear madam, it is so very large a majority of your fellow countrymen that are of this insignificant stamp."

Rather similarly in *Janet's Repentance*, but this time the author parades a character:

"And who is this bright-looking woman . . . ? Can it be Janet Dempster, on whom we looked with such deep pity, one sad midnight, hardly a fortnight ago? Yes . . ."

The *Scenes* abound in this obvious solicitation of sympathy or admiration for hero or heroine. The prose becomes highly yet weakly emotional:

"Soothing, unspeakable charm of gentle womanhood! . . . Happy the man, you would have thought, whose eye will rest on her in the pauses of his fireside reading—whose hot aching forehead will be soothed by the contact of her cool soft hand . . ."

The constituent elements of these stories fall into neat divisions. There are general passages, in which there is often more whimsicality than thought; then the comic relief of rural characters (despite George Eliot's professed aim of sympathetic understanding and unflinching realism); then the pathetic scenes, of which Milly's deathbed is the first and probably best known. Sir Leslie Stephen (in his biography in the *English Men of Letters* Series) objected to

the parade of children before the dying woman: the language reinforces his objection:

"The mother motioned with her pallid lips for the dear child to lean towards her and kiss her; and then Patty's great anguish overcame her, and she burst into sobs."

Contemporaries found no sentimentality in George Eliot: this is not surprising after Little Em'ly; but a comparison of the earlier and later work makes clear the comparative sickliness of the earlier pathos.

Then there are descriptions, carefully detailed, emotionally charged, and not very original; and psychological passages in which processes of thought are painstakingly yet sympathetically reproduced. It is clear already that George Eliot has great powers, but they are not yet integrated into a style expressive of achieved personality.

2

Adam Bede followed the *Scenes*, in 1859, and was widely popular at once. The reasons for its appeal are easy to analyse: they are, briefly, its evangelical note, its old England of beef and beer, and the strong—and, for the times, "daring"—"human interest" of the story of Hetty: excellent ingredients for a Victorian best-seller. For our present purpose, we may neglect all the usual critical questions, as to whether Dinah is the real heroine, and so on. The important point for George Eliot's development, is that she had here a "powerful" story in which she was interested, and a story about simple people. Greater interest in the subject matter caused her to write more on the level of events; i.e., she relies mainly for her effect upon the events themselves, recording them in ordinary language, usually devoid of the embroidery of whimsical or moral asides characteristic of the *Scenes of Clerical Life*:

"For the first few miles out of Stoniton she walked on bravely, always fixing on some tree or gate or projecting bush at the most distant visible point in the road as a goal, and feeling a faint joy when she had reached it. But when she came to the fourth milestone, the first she had happened to notice among the long grass by the roadside, and read that she was only four miles beyond Stoniton, her courage sank."

Compared with the highly "literary" style of much of the *Scenes of Clerical Life*, this is more than an advance: it is a new beginning. There is great gain in simplicity and freedom from artificial posturing, but there is a corresponding loss in allusiveness.

A Victorian novel is a long, unwieldy affair, however, and in other parts the old blemishes are in evidence. Mrs. Poyser is more fully a "character" than Sam Weller, but she *is* rather Dickensian, and still serves mainly as comic interlude. Descriptions of the countryside are simple and fairly vivid, though deviating very little from the stock Victorian epithets (rural scenes are not George Eliot's strong point, despite the critics) ; and the psychology of Hetty is well presented in the form of her own reflections upon incidents and people. This concreteness is usually preferred to George Eliot's later use of abstract exposition, but comparatively it possesses the disadvantages of diffusiveness, inexactitude, and, more subtly, of limiting the reader's view to the actual person under discussion. We come very close to Hetty's mind in *Adam Bede,* but in *Daniel Deronda* we are made to understand Gwendolen Harleth in her social environment and in her universal significance.

The chapter "In which the Story pauses a little" shows slight advance on *Amos Barton;* and some passages about Hetty can be very trying:

"Ah, what a prize the man gets who wins a sweet bride like Hetty! How the men envy him who come to the wedding breakfast, and see her hanging on his arm in her white lace and orange blossoms. The dear, young, round, soft, flexible thing! Her heart must be just as soft, her temper just as free from angles, her character just as pliant."

The fact that this is meant satirically hardly excuses it.

The "merry England" element is equally immature. It is to be found in the feasting at the Hall, the farm supper, in various asides throughout, and notably at the end of Chapter LII :

"Old leisure was quite a different personage; he read only one newspaper, innocent of leaders, and was free from that periodicity of sensations which we call post time. He was a contemplative, rather stout gentleman, of excellent digestion: happy in his inability to know the causes of things, preferring the things themselves . . . he had an easy, jolly conscience, broad-backed like himself, and able to carry a great deal of beer or port-wine— not being made squeamish by doubts and qualms and lofty aspirations."

Compare the following, from *Middlemarch:*

"The men of Frick were not ill-fed, and were less given to fanaticism than to a strong muscular suspicion; less inclined to believe that they were peculiarly cared for by heaven, than to regard heaven itself as rather disposed to take them in— a disposition observable in the weather."

The personification of "Old leisure," her tacit approval of the good old times, has given way to a cool estimate of their limitations. Stylistically, it is interesting to contrast the phrase, "conscience, broad-backed like himself," with its later parallel, "a strong muscular suspicion," at once more compact and much more widely allusive.

The Mill on the Floss shows only the slightest advance in integration. It is partly straightforward narrative and dialogue, like much of *Adam Bede:* but the autobiographical element introduces a subtler treatment of character, in a discursive, whimsical style (counterpoising self-pity), somewhat like the *Scenes of Clerical Life,* but with less straining for literary effect.

Silas Marner, however, is simply told and suffers less from sentimentality and pretentious asides, though the plot itself is mechanically worked out:

42   Discussions of George Eliot

"In the early ages of the world, we know, it was believed that each territory was inhabited and ruled by its own divinities, so that a man could cross the bordering heights and be out of the reach of his native gods, whose presence was confined to the streams and the groves and the hills among which he had lived from his birth. And poor Silas was vaguely conscious of something not unlike the feeling of primitive men, when they fled thus, in fear or in sullenness, from the face of an unpropitious deity."

It is severely simple, balanced, devoid of the earlier "cleverness" or emotionalism, and begins a purgation which *Romola* almost completed.

3

According to Mathilde Blind, George Eliot succeeded so well in suggesting the Italian atmosphere in *Romola,* that Italians recognised their national characteristics in its psychology: according to Sir Leslie Stephen, this was only Italian politeness. However this may be, the choice of theme was fortunate for George Eliot's development. It took her away at last from childhood reminiscence and its attendant dangers. First, the "tone" is different: the cultivated reader may also know a fair amount about fifteenth-century Florence, and a dignified equality takes the place of emotional entreaties for indulgence or clever parading of specialized local knowledge. Secondly, the attitude towards the subject is also more satisfactory. Hitherto she has been dealing with characters of inferior culture to herself, and the best writers find it difficult to avoid patronage in such circumstances. We know that George Eliot was in frequent despair over *Romola*, and no doubt the experience did her good. There is a considerable display of erudition, but it is never of that insulting type which greatly exceeds the dignity of its object.

It is in *Romola*, too, that she achieves the level of abstraction which best suits her. Description is minimized, and external events merely noticed as leading to or resulting from the mental events which are her main concern. Dramatic effect is ruthlessly sacrificed, the most telling scenes are never written, or are written with philosophical calm (the phrase is literally justified) : the eye is always on the object, and the object is always a mental state. Here is a sentence to which Sir Leslie Stephen takes exception as "an almost Germanic concatenation of clauses":

"Not that Savonarola had uttered and written a falsity when he declared his belief in a future supernatural attestation of his work; but his mind was so constituted that while it was easy for him to believe in a miracle which, being distant and undefined, was screened behind the strong reasons he saw for its occurrence, and yet easier for him to have a belief in inward miracles such as his own prophetic inspiration and divinely-wrought intuitions, it was at the same time insurmountably difficult to him to believe in the probability of a miracle which, like this of being carried unhurt through the fire, pressed in all its details on his imagination and involved a demand not only for belief but for exceptional action."

Sir Leslie Stephen further comments:

"Savonarola's mind was surely, in this respect, like most people's; we all think that we can bear the dentist's forceps till we get into his armchair,"

which shows how the most careful statement can be misconstrued when good will is wanting. The advantage of involved sentences is twofold: subordinate clauses place the constituent ideas in clearer relations of relative importance, so that thought becomes a structure and not a stream; and further, the necessity of slower reading is enforced by the style.

The passage quoted above naturally brings to mind George Eliot's various reading: she was the most scholarly of Victorian novelists, and her mature style—when she had lived down the lively contrast of writing novels and translating theology—owes much to her close reading of seventeenth and eighteenth century divines. *Romola* may be somewhat dry, but there is a new solidity, integrity, and restraint in the balanced sentences, which, combined with other elements, leads on to the success of *Middlemarch* and *Daniel Deronda.*

Again, though attention has been diverted from objects as such, they are beginning to reappear, sparsely as yet, in the form of simile or metaphor:

"Any maxims that required a man to fling away the good that was needed to make existence sweet, were only the lining of human selfishness turned outward."

There is perhaps less strain in comparing the "ravell'd sleave of care," than in the more popular comparison between George Eliot and Shakespeare in respect of "characters."

The choice of an historical theme was certainly valuable in some fundamental respects, but it is also the cause of a certain thinness in the prose, not observable before or since. Fifteenth-century Florence could be approached *via* the best authors; therefore its virtues shone: and its vices were more tolerable through distance. George Eliot knew the dissoluteness of the times— and shows she knew it—as an intellectual fact; but she did not flog dead horses. So that there is only an occasional note of satire, when a social disease common to all ages is touched on (e.g. the entry of the French king into Florence, or the supper in the Rucellai gardens) ; and descriptive epithets are usually non-committal. A good half of her distinctive powers lay dormant.

4

Felix Holt shows signs of mental indigestion, and it is not until *Middlemarch* that the Florentine purgation has full effect. But in *Middlemarch* her style is achieved. In a novel of this type, complete stylistic uniformity is impossible and undesirable: there are passages in which the dominant note is satirical, others of almost pure psychological analysis, and others, again, in which pathos is entirely unrelieved. But at each particular point the total theme is

in evidence: there is nothing like the hotch-potch of the earlier novels, in which passages of purely humorous intention alternate with passages in which the pathos is underlined by the writer's unreserved participation in the feelings of her characters: in *Middlemarch* the intention, and the attitude towards the subject, are serious throughout, even in the light glancing at social follies. As in *Romola,* the attention is usually at the level of mental events. There are few descriptions of the country-side or of interiors, and such as there are, are strictly utilitarian in intention: the outward appearance of a character is summarized at once and left alone, excepting where, as in the case of Rosamond Vincy, it is of extrinsic importance. Even then the description is not mainly in terms of sensory fact, so as to arouse admiration (cf. Hetty), but in such terms as to present its social and ethical significance. Here is the paragraph in which Rosamond is introduced:

"Old provincial society had its share of this subtle movement: had not only its striking downfalls, its brilliant young professional dandies who ended by living up an entry with a drab and six children for their establishment, but also those less marked vicissitudes which are constantly shifting the boundaries of social intercourse, and begetting new consciousness of interdependence. Some slipped a little downward, some got higher footing: people denied aspirates, gained wealth, and fastidious gentlemen stood for boroughs; some were caught in political currents, some in ecclesiastical, and perhaps found themselves surprisingly grouped in consequence; while a few personages or families that stood with rocky firmness amid all this fluctuation, were slowly presenting new aspects in spite of solidity, and altering with the double change of self and beholder. Municipal town and rural parish gradually made fresh threads of connexion—gradually, as the old stocking gave way to the savings-bank, and the worship of the solar guinea became extinct; while squires and baronets, and even lords who had once lived blamelessly afar from the civic mind, gathered the faultiness of closer acquaintanceship. Settlers, too, came from distant counties, some with an alarming novelty of skill, others with an offensive advantage in cunning. In fact, much the same movement and mixture went on in old England as we find in older Herodotus, who also, in telling what had been, thought it well to take a woman's lot for his starting-point; though Io, as a maiden apparently beguiled by attractive merchandise, was the reverse of Miss Brooke, and in this respect perhaps bore more resemblance to Rosamond Vincy, who had excellent taste in costume, with that nymph-like figure and pure blondness which give the largest range to choice in the flow and colour of drapery. But these things made only part of her charm. She was admitted to be the flower of Mrs. Lemon's school, the chief school in the county, where the teaching included all that was demanded in the accomplished female—even to extras, such as the getting in and out of a carriage. Mrs. Lemon herself had always held up Miss Vincy as an example: no pupil, she said, exceeded that young lady for mental acquisition and propriety of speech, while her musical execution was quite exceptional. We cannot help the way in which people speak of us, and probably if Mrs. Lemon had undertaken to describe Juliet or Imogen, these heroines would not have seemed poetical. The first vision of Rosamond would have been enough with most judges to dispel any prejudice excited by Mrs. Lemon's praise."

This passage is worth studying, and contrasting with the opening paragraph of the *Scenes of Clerical Life,* quoted above. The tone is easy, yet dignified and restrained. There is no merely verbal humour, no striving to be "literary," no grandiose or sentimental rhythms. The general air is of quiet statement. The complex sentence-form first noticed in connexion with *Romola,* is the basis of this mature style; but it is much altered. There is reminiscence of the eighteenth century: "She was admitted to be the flower of Mrs. Lemon's school, the chief school in the county, where the teaching included all that was demanded of the accomplished female . . ."; and of the seventeenth: "Some slipped a little downward, some got higher footing: people denied aspirates, gained wealth . . ." (cf. Earle). Terse, tight-packed meaning has succeeded barren abstractions, within the same form. The abstract noun is still used for conven-

ience ("consciousness of independence"), but the world of sense, banished from direct contemplation, returns in simile and metaphor and concrete example, so that, though the level of attention remains the same as in *Romola,* there is a sense of fulness in *Middlemarch,* directly derivable from the style. In the phrase, "rocky firmness amid all this fluctuation," the adjective "rocky" restores to "fluctuation" its metaphorical force. The rhythms and language of common speech lend variety to the balanced sentence-structure: "living up an entry with a drab and six children."

The satiric wit derives its effect from compression (apparently heterogeneous ideas are yoked together apparently by violence; but sharp surprise is followed by agreement) and from judgements of value constantly implied: "even lords who had once lived blamelessly afar from the civic mind, gathered the faultiness of closer acquaintanceship. Settlers, too, came from distant counties, some with an alarming novelty of skill, others with an offensive advantage in cunning."

Note the use of balance in the last two phrases, in adding to the satiric effect. This is highly conscious art, but there is nothing meretricious about it: in the mature George Eliot, words are never employed for their own sake; they are always as nearly as possible plate glass to the ideas behind them.

The introduction of Rosamond Vincy is casual, in the middle of a general summary of changing social conditions; and her description at the same time develops the general theme, and shows her as a product of the conditions just presented: which is doing on the level of prose technique what the whole novel does on the higher level of mental events. The "nymph-like figure and pure blondness" is intentionally featureless; and, in the next phrase, the value of these attributes is put on a par with the value of a dressmaker's block: this phrase is very subtly differentiated into satire by the commercial "largest range to choice."

There are other characteristics of style not represented in this passage, but which deserve mention. Occasional epigrams had always illuminated George Eliot's writing: as early as *Amos Barton* we have a favourite:

"Every man who is not a monster, a mathematician, or a mad philosopher, is the slave of some woman or other."

This scarcely bears examination (the alliteration renders it suspect from the start); and perhaps a number of the "Wise, Witty, and Tender Sayings" culled from George Eliot, are of this order. But the integrity of *Middlemarch* extends even to its epigrams, which, also, since the surrounding style is epigrammatic, do not distract admiring attention towards the author—the usual effect, and purpose, of such stylistic adornments. Just above the paragraph we have quoted, is an example:

"Destiny stands by sarcastic with our *dramatis personae* folded in her hand."

The context saves it from being taken too seriously and so condemned as pretentious.

Scientific metaphors and similes contribute to the clinical effect of psychological analysis, though the "science," as well as its application, is frequently reminiscent of the early seventeenth century:

". . . prejudices, like odorous bodies, have a double existence both solid and subtle—solid as the pyramids, subtle as the twentieth echo of an echo, or as the memory of hyacinths which once scented the darkness. And Will was of a temperament to feel keenly the presence of subtleties . . ."

Not only "odorous bodies," but pyramids, echoes, and hyacinths: it is in this way that the world of sense comes back into intellectual constructions. Observe also the rapid change of feeling between the clinical, Brunonian beginning, and the restrainedly "Romantic" end, of the first sentence.

The writing is individual, not in the sense of expressing personal peculiarities (like Lamb's Essays), but in the sense that each word is individually selected for its purpose, whereas most writers content themselves usually with the phrase to hand:

"It was not in Dorothea's nature, for more than the duration of a paroxysm, to sit in the narrow cell of her calamity, in the besotted misery of a consciousness that only sees another's lot as an accident of its own."

George Eliot was a very subtle analyst of that part of the mind which is concerned with good and evil, particularly in those unusual people who possess a true "inner life" of spiritual aspiration. In the early novels, her characters were without culture, but from *Romola* onwards she concerned herself with spiritual aspiration in minds of good general culture, and, after *Romola,* in relation to an alien environment. This called out all her resources, and the resultant impression is of the author's self-forgetfulness in the face of an important task. Yet there is an air of mastery in *Romola, Middlemarch,* and *Daniel Deronda*—not the easy mastery which a "philosophical" author secures through an oversimplification of life; but the matured power which can accept mysteries, and can accept disillusionments without clamour. The *Spectator,* says Sir Leslie Stephen, in reviewing *Middlemarch* described George Eliot as "the most melancholy of authors": her penetration jarred upon nineteenth-century self-esteem. . . .

F. R. Leavis

George Eliot

THERE is general agreement that an appraisal of George Eliot must be a good deal preoccupied with major discriminations—that the body of her work exhibits within itself striking differences not merely of kind, but between the more and the less satisfactory, and exhibits them in such a way that the history of her art has to be seen as something less happy in its main lines than just an unfolding of her genius, a prosperous development of her distinctive powers, with growing maturity. It is generally assumed that this aspect of her performance is significantly related to the fact of her having displayed impressive intellectual gifts outside her art, so that she was a distinguished figure in the world of Herbert Spencer and the *Westminster Review* before she became a novelist. And there is something like a unanimity to the effect that it is distinctive of her, among great novelists, to be peculiarly addicted to moral preoccupations.

The force of this last—what it amounts to or intends, and the significance it has for criticism—is elusive; and it seems well to start with a preliminary glance at what, from his hours with the critics, the reader is likely to recall as a large established blur across the field of vision. Henry James seems to me to have shown finer intelligence than anyone else in writing about George Eliot, and he, in his review of the Cross *Life* of her, tells us that, for her, the novel "was not primarily a picture of life, capable of deriving a high value from its form, but a moralized fable, the last word of a philosophy endeavouring to teach by example." The blur is seen here in that misleading antithesis, which, illusory as it is,

James's commentary insists on. What, we ask, is the "form" from which a "picture of life" derives its value? As we should expect, the term "aesthetic," with its trail of confusion, turns up in the neighbourhood (it is a term the literary critic would do well to abjure). James notes, as characterizing "that side of George Eliot's nature which was weakest," the "absence of free aesthetic life," and he says that her "figures and situations" are "not *seen* in the irresponsible plastic way." But, we ask, in what great, in what interesting, novel *are* the figures and situations seen in an "irresponsible plastic way" (a useful determination of one of the intentions of "aesthetic")? Is there any great novelist whose preoccupation with "form" is not a matter of his responsibility towards a rich human interest, or complexity of interests, profoundly realized?—a responsibility involving, of its very nature, imaginative sympathy, moral discrimination and judgment of relative human value? . . .

The large discrimination generally made in respect of George Eliot is a simple one. Henry James's account is subtler than any other I know, but isn't worked out to consistency. He says (though the generalization is implicitly criticized by the context, being inadequate to his perception):

"We feel in her, always, that she proceeds from the abstract to the concrete; that her figures and situations are evolved, as the phrase is, from her moral consciousness, and are only indirectly the products of observation."

What this gives us is, according to the accepted view, one half of her—the unsatisfactory half. The great George Eliot, ac-

From *The Great Tradition*, New York, Doubleday Anchor Books, 1954. Reprinted by permission.

cording to this view, is the novelist of reminiscence; the George Eliot who writes out of her memories of childhood and youth, renders the poignancy and charm of personal experience, and gives us, in a mellow light, the England of her young days, and of the days then still alive in family tradition. Her classics are *Scenes of Clerical Life*, *Adam Bede*, *The Mill on the Floss*, and *Silas Marner*. With these books she exhausted her material, and in order to continue a novelist had to bring the other half of herself into play—to hand over, in fact, to the intellectual. *Romola* is the product of an exhausting and misguided labour of excogitation and historical reconstruction (a judgment no one is likely to dispute). *Felix Holt* and *Daniel Deronda* also represent the distinguished intellectual rather than the great novelist; in them she "proceeds from the abstract to the concrete," "her figures and situations are evolved from her moral consciousness," they "are deeply studied and massively supported, but . . ."—Henry James's phrases fairly convey the accepted view.

It should be said at once that he is not to be identified with it (he discriminates firmly, for instance, in respect of *Daniel Deronda*). Still, he expresses for us admirably what has for long been the current idea of her development, and he does in such passages as this endorse the view that, in the later novels, the intellectual gets the upper hand:

"The truth is, perception and reflection at the outset divided George Eliot's great talent between them; but as time went on circumstances led the latter to develop itself at the expense of the former—one of these circumstances being apparently the influence of George Henry Lewes."

And we don't feel that he is inclined to dissociate himself to any significant extent when, in the *Conversation* about *Daniel Deronda*, he makes Constantius say:

"She strikes me as a person who certainly has naturally a taste for general considerations, but who has fallen upon an age and a circle which

have compelled her to give them an exaggerated attention. She does not strike me as naturally a critic, less still as naturally a sceptic; her spontaneous part is to observe life and to feel it—to feel it with admirable depth. Contemplation, sympathy and faith—something like that, I should say, would have been her natural scale."

At any rate, that gives what appears to be still the established notion of George Eliot.

It will have been noted above that I left out *Middlemarch*. And it will have been commented that *Middlemarch*, which, with *Felix Holt* between, comes in order of production after *Romola* and doesn't at all represent a reversion to the phase of "spontaneity," has for at least two decades been pretty generally acclaimed as one of the great masterpieces of English fiction. That is true. Virginia Woolf, a good index of cultivated acceptance in that period, writes (in *The Common Reader*, first series) :

"It is not that her power diminishes, for, to our thinking, it is at its highest in the mature *Middlemarch*, the magnificent book which, with all its imperfections, is one of the few English novels written for grown-up people."

This judgment, in a characteristic and not very satisfactory essay on George Eliot, must be set to Mrs. Woolf's credit as a critic; there is no doubt that it has had a good deal to do with the established recognition of *Middlemarch*.

But Mrs. Woolf makes no serious attempt at the work of general revision such a judgment implies, and the appreciation of George Eliot's *œuvre* has not been put on a critical basis and reduced to consistency. For if you think so highly of *Middlemarch*, then, to be consistent, you must be more qualified in your praise of the early things than persisting convention recognizes. Isn't there, in fact, a certain devaluing to be done? The key word in that sentence quoted from Mrs. Woolf is "mature." Her distinguished father (whose book on George Eliot in *The English Men of Letters* has his characteristic virtues) supplies, where their popularity is concerned, the key word

48   Discussions of George Eliot

for the earlier works when he speaks of a "loss of charm" involved in her development after *The Mill on the Floss*. At the risk of appearing priggish one may suggest that there is a tendency to overrate charm. Certainly charm is overrated when it is preferred to maturity. . . .

If we hesitated to judge that in *Romola* George Eliot "proceeds from the abstract to the concrete" it would be because "proceed" might seem to imply "attain." Of this monument of excogitation and reconstruction Henry James himself says: "More than any of her novels it was evolved from her moral consciousness—a moral consciousness encircled by a prodigious amount of literary research." The "figures and situations" are indeed "deeply studied and massively supported," and they represent characteristic preoccupations of the novelist, but they fail to emerge from the state of generalized interest: they are not brought to any sharp edge of realization. Tito Melema, developing a mere mild insufficiency of positive unselfishness into a positive and lethal viciousness, illustrates a favourite theme, moral and psychological, but he remains an illustration, thought of, thought out, and painstakingly specified; never becoming anything like a prior reality that embodies the theme and presents it as life. The analogous and worse failure in respect of Savonarola is fairly suggested by such passages of laborious analytic prose as Leslie Stephen quotes (*George Eliot,* p. 134), with the comment:

"this almost Germanic concatenation of clauses not only puts such obvious truths languidly, but keeps Savonarola himself at a distance. We are not listening to a Hamlet, but to a judicious critic analysing the state of mind which prompts 'to be or not to be.' "

—There is no presence, that is; the analysis serves instead.

Romola herself Leslie Stephen judges more favourably—indeed, very favourably. And it is true that she represents something other than the failure of a powerful

mind to warm analysis into creation; she is a palpably emotional presence: Romola, in fact, is another idealized George Eliot—less real than Maggie Tulliver and more idealized. While patrician and commandingly beautiful, she has also George Eliot's combination of intellectual power, emancipation, inherent piety, and hunger for exaltations.

"The pressing problem for Romola just then was . . . to keep alive that flame of unselfish emotion by which a life of sadness might still be a life of active love."

—With "Maggie" substituted for "Romola," that might have come as a patently autobiographical note from *The Mill on the Floss*. And it is the immediate presence of the yearning translator of Strauss that we feel in such situations as this:

"Romola, kneeling with buried face on the altar step, was enduring one of those sickening moments when the enthusiasm which had come to her as the only energy strong enough to make life worthy, seemed to be inevitably bound up with vain dreams and wilful eye-shutting."

And when we read that "tender fellow-feeling for the nearest has its danger too, and is apt to be timid and sceptical towards the larger aims without which life cannot rise into religion" we know that we are in direct contact with the "pressing problem" of the nineteenth-century intellectual, contemporary of Mill, Matthew Arnold and Comte. So that we can hardly help being pryingly personal in our conjectures when, going on, we read:

"No one who has ever known what it is thus to lose faith in a fellow man whom he has profoundly loved and reverenced, will lightly say that the shock can leave the faith in the Invisible Goodness unshaken. With the sinking of high human trust, the dignity of life sinks too: we cease to believe in our own better self, since that also is part of the common nature which is degraded in our thought; and all the finer impulses of the soul are dulled."

—Dr. John Chapman? we ask.

The answer, of course, doesn't matter. The point we have to make is that this closeness of relation between heroine and author is no more here than elsewhere in George Eliot a strength. Romola, in fact, has none of the reality associated with Maggie Tulliver, but she brings in the weakness, associated with Maggie, that embarrasses us in *The Mill on the Floss*.

The passage just quoted opens the episode in which Romola, lying down in an open boat, abandons herself to the winds and tides—"To be freed from the burden of choice when all motive was bruised, to commit herself, sleeping, to destiny which would either bring death or else new necessities that might rouse a new life in her." "Had she," she asks, as she lies in the gliding boat, "found anything like the dream of her girlhood? No." But she is to find now, in alleged actuality, something embarrassingly like a girlhood dream. She drifts ashore at the plague-stricken village, and, a ministering Madonna—"the Mother with the glory about her tending the sick"—is a miracle for the villagers. It is a miracle for her too, rescuing her from her "pressing problem" with a "flame of unselfish emotion," provided by a heaven-sent chance out of the void.

Few will want to read *Romola* a second time, and few can ever have got through it once without some groans. It is indubitably the work of a very gifted mind, but of a mind misusing itself; and it is the one novel answering to the kind of account of George Eliot that became current during the swing of the pendulum against her after her death.

Yet *Romola* has habitually been included in the lists of cheap reprints, and probably a good many more readers have tackled it than have ever taken up *Felix Holt*. In writing *Felix Holt*, which brings us back to England, George Eliot did look up *The Times* for 1830 or thereabouts; but there was no tremendous and exhausting labour of historical reconstruction. What called for the most uncongenial hard work on her part was the elaboration of the plot—work (it strikes us to-day) about as perversely, if not as desiccatingly, misdirected as that which went to evoking life at Florence in the time of Savonarola. The complications of the thorough-paced Victorian plot depend, with painful correctness (professional advice having been taken of the Positivist friend, Frederic Harrison), on some esoteric subtleties of the law of entail, and they demand of the reader a strenuousness of attention that, if he is an admirer of George Eliot, he is unwilling to devote.

It is in the theme represented by the title of the book that the "reflective" preponderance of the "moral consciousness," working from the "abstract" without being able to turn it into convincing perception, notably manifests itself. Felix Holt is the ideal working man. Though educated, he is wholly loyal to his class (to the extent of remaining shaggy in appearance and manners), and dedicates his life to its betterment; but, while proposing to take an active part in politics, he refuses to countenance any of the compromises of organized political action. He denounces the Radical agent for fighting the constituency in the usual way. Rational appeal to unalloyed principle—that alone can be permitted; the time-honoured methods of party warfare, defended as practical necessities for party success, debase and betray the people's cause, and there must be no truck with them. Felix is as noble and courageous in act as in ideal, and is wholly endorsed by his creator. That in presenting these unrealities George Eliot gives proof of a keen interest in political, social and economic history, and in the total complex movement of civilization, and exhibits an impressive command of the facts, would seem to confirm the deprecatory view commonly taken of the relation between intellectual and novelist. Here is the way Felix Holt, Radical, talks:

" 'Oh, yes, your ringed and scented men of the people!—I won't be one of them. Let a man throttle himself with a satin stock, and he'll get new wants and new motives. Metamorphosis will have begun at his neckjoint, and it will go on till it has changed his likings first and then his reasoning, which will follow his likings as the feet of a hungry dog follow his nose. I'll have none of your clerkly gentility. I might end by collecting greasy pence from poor men to buy myself a fine coat and a glutton's dinner, on pretence of serving the poor men. I'd sooner be Paley's fat pigeon than a demagogue all tongue and stomach, though'—here Felix changed his voice a little—'I should like well enough to be another sort of demagogue, if I could.'

" 'Then you have a strong interest in the great political movements of these times?' said Mr. Lyon, with a perceptible flashing of the eyes.

" 'I should think so. I despise every man who has not—or, having it, doesn't try to rouse it in other men.' "

The consequences of general intention combined with inexperience are disastrously plain. The idealizing bent seen to be so marked in Adam Bede when we compare him with Caleb Garth of *Middlemarch* is not really a strength; but George Eliot knew the country artisan at first hand and intimately. In offering to present the Dignity of Labour in the ideal town working-man she is relying on her "moral consciousness" unqualified by first-hand knowledge.

Felix Holt's very unideal mother, though not the same kind of disaster (she's only a minor figure, of course), is not much more convincing; she seems to be done out of Dickens rather than from life. The Reverend Rufus Lyon, the Congregationalist minister, heroically quaint reminder of the heroic age of Puritanism (and inspired, one guesses, by Scott), is incredible and a bore—to say which is a severe criticism, since his talk occupies a large proportion of the book. Esther, the beautiful and elegant young lady passing as his daughter, is interesting only in relation to other feminine studies of the author's, and to her treatment in general of feminine charm.

But there is an element in the novel as yet untouched on. It is represented by this,

where the dialogue is so different in quality from that in which Felix Holt figures, and the analysis of so different an order (and in so different a prose) from that characteristic of *Romola*:

" 'Harold is remarkably acute and clever,' he began at last, since Mrs. Transome did not speak. 'If he gets into Parliament, I have no doubt he will distinguish himself. He has a quick eye for business of all kinds.'

" 'That is no comfort to me,' said Mrs. Transome. To-day she was more conscious than usual of that bitterness which was always in her mind in Jermyn's presence, but which was carefully suppressed because she could not endure the degradation she inwardly felt should ever become visible or audible in acts or words of her own—should ever be reflected in any word or look of his. For years there had been a deep silence about the past between them: on her side, because she remembered; on his, because he more and more forgot.

" 'I trust he is not unkind to you in any way. I know his opinions pain you; but I trust you find him in everything else disposed to be a good son.'

" 'Oh, to be sure—good as men are disposed to be to women, giving them cushions and carriages, and recommending them to enjoy themselves, and then expecting them to be contented under contempt and neglect. I have no power over him—remember that—none.'

"Jermyn turned to look in Mrs. Transome's face: it was long since he had heard her speak to him as if she were losing her self-command.

" 'Has he shown any unpleasant feeling about your management of the affairs?'

" '*My* management of the affairs!' Mrs. Transome said, with concentrated rage, flashing a fierce look at Jermyn. She checked herself: she felt as if she were lighting a torch to flare on her own past folly and misery. It was a resolve which had become a habit, that she would never quarrel with this man—never tell him what she saw him to be. She had kept her woman's pride and sensibility intact: through all her life there had vibrated the maiden need to have her hand kissed and be the object of chivalry. And so she sank into silence again, trembling.

"Jermyn felt annoyed—nothing more. There was nothing in his mind corresponding to the intricate meshes of sensitiveness in Mrs. Transome's. He was anything but stupid; yet he always blundered when he wanted to be delicate or magnanimous; he constantly sought to soothe others by praising himself. Moral vulgarity cleaved to him like an hereditary odour. He blundered now.

" 'My dear Mrs. Transome,' he said, in a tone of bland kindness, 'you are agitated—you appear angry with me. Yet I think, if you consider, you will see that you have nothing to complain of in me, unless you will complain of the inevitable course of man's life. I have always met your wishes both in happy circumstances and in unhappy ones. I should be ready to do so now, if it were possible.'

"Every sentence was as pleasant to her as if it had been cut in her bared arm. Some men's kindness and love-making are more exasperating, more humiliating than others' derision, but the pitiable woman who has once made herself secretly dependent on a man who is beneath her in feeling must bear that humiliation for fear of worse. Coarse kindness is at least better than coarse anger; and in all private quarrels the duller nature is triumphant by reason of its dulness. Mrs. Transome knew in her inmost soul that those relations which had sealed her lips on Jermyn's conduct in business matters, had been with him a ground for presuming that he should have impunity in any lax dealing into which circumstances had led him. She knew that she herself had endured all the more privation because of his dishonest selfishness. And now, Harold's long-deferred heirship, and his return with startlingly unexpected penetration, activity, and assertion of mastery, had placed them both in the full presence of a difficulty which had been prepared by the years of vague uncertainty as to issues."

It should be plain from the quality of this that the theme it handles is profoundly felt and sharply realized. This theme concerns Mrs. Transome, her son Harold, and the family lawyer, Matthew Jermyn. It is utterly different in kind from anything else in *Felix Holt* and from anything earlier of George Eliot's, and when we come to it we see finally that Henry James's antithesis, "perspective" and "reflective," will not do. For if we ask how this art is so astonishingly finer and maturer than anything George Eliot had done before, the answer is in terms of a perception that is so much more clear and profound because the perceiving focuses the profound ex-

perience of years—experience worked over by reflective thought, and so made capable of focusing. What we perceive depends on what we bring to the perceiving; and George Eliot brought a magnificent intelligence, functioning here as mature understanding. Intelligence in her was not always worsted by emotional needs; the relation between the artist and the intellectual in her (with the formidable "exemption from cerebral lassitude") was not always a matter of her intellect being enlisted in the service of her immaturity.

The beneficent relation between artist and intellectual is to be seen in the new impersonality of the Transome theme. The theme is realized with an intensity certainly not inferior to that of the most poignant autobiographical places in George Eliot, but the directly personal vibration—the directly personal engagement of the novelist —that we feel in Maggie Tulliver's intensities even at their most valid is absent here. "The more perfect the artist, the more completely separate in him will be the man who suffers and the mind which creates": it is in the part of *Felix Holt* dealing with Mrs. Transome that George Eliot becomes one of the great creative artists. She has not here, it will be noted, a heroine with whom she can be tempted to identify herself. Mrs. Transome is County, and how unlike she is to the novelist appears sufficiently in this account of her:

"She had that high-born imperious air which would have marked her as an object of hatred and reviling by a revolutionary mob. Her person was too typical of social distinctions to be passed by with indifference by anyone: it would have fitted an empress in her own right, who had had to rule in spite of faction, to dare the violation of treaties and dread retributive invasions, to grasp after new territories, to be defiant in desperate circumstances, and to feel a woman's hunger of the heart for ever unsatisfied. . . . When she was young she had been thought wonderfully clever and accomplished, and had been rather ambitious of intellectual superiority—had secretly picked out for private reading the lighter parts of dangerous French authors—and in company had been able to talk of Mr. Burke's style, or of Chateaubriand's eloquence—had laughed at the Lyrical Ballads and admired Mr. Southey's Thalaba. She always thought that the dangerous French authors were wicked and that her reading of them was a sin; but many sinful things were highly agreeable to her, and many things which she did not doubt to be good and true were dull and meaningless. She found ridicule of Biblical characters very amusing, and she was interested in stories of illicit passion; but she believed all the while that truth and safety lay in due attendance on prayers and sermons, in the admirable doctrines and ritual of the Church of England, equally remote from Puritanism and Popery; in fact, in such a view of this world and the next as would preserve the existing arrangements of English society quite unshaken, keeping down the obtrusiveness of the vulgar and the discontent of the poor."

The treatment of Mrs. Transome is not, as this description may suggest, ironical. The irony, a tragic irony, resides in her situation, which is presented with complete objectivity—though with poignant sympathy, unlike as her strains and distresses are to the novelist's own. In this sympathy there is not a trace of self-pity or self-indulgence. Mrs. Transome is a study in Nemesis. And, although her case is conceived in an imagination that is profoundly moral, the presentment of it is a matter of psychological observation—psychological observation so utterly convincing in its significance that the price paid by Mrs. Transome for her sin in inevitable consequences doesn't need a moralist's insistence, and there is none; to speak of George Eliot here as a moralist would, one feels, be to misplace a stress. She is simply a great artist—a great novelist, with a great novelist's psychological insight and fineness of human valuation. Here is one aspect of Mrs. Transome's tragedy:

"The mother's love is at first an absorbing delight, blunting all other sensibilities; it is an expansion of the animal existence; it enlarges the imagined range for self to move in: but in after years it can only continue to be joy on the same terms as other long-lived love—that is, by much

suppression of self, and power of living in the experience of another. Mrs. Transome had darkly felt the pressure of that unchangeable fact. Yet she had clung to the belief that somehow the possession of this son was the best thing she lived for; to believe otherwise would have made her memory too ghastly a companion."

Mrs. Transome, of course, is not capable of recognizing the "unchangeable fact" of which she "darkly feels the pressure." She cannot alter herself, and for her the worth and meaning of life lie in command, and the imposition of her will. This is shown to us, not with any incitement to censure, but as making her, in its inevitable consequences, tragically pitiable. For her feeble-minded husband she can feel little but contempt. That the unsatisfactory elder son who took after him is dead is matter for rejoicing: Harold, the second and quite other son, now becomes the heir, and, returning home from the Levant where he has made a fortune, will be able to put the encumbered family estate on a new footing, so that, belatedly, the lady of Transome Court will assume real dominion, and take her due place in the County. That dream, for many starved years the reason for living, dies as soon as they meet, and the despairing bitterness that engulfs her as she realizes that he is indeed her son,[1] and that for him too command and the exercise of will are the meaning of life, is evoked (notably in the exchanges with Denner, her maid) with an astringently moving power unsurpassed in literature.

To the tormenting frustration and hopelessness is soon added fear. It is not only that Harold, with his poised kindness that is so utterly unaware of her, frustrates her social hopes by proclaiming himself a

[1] "Under the shock of discovering her son's Radicalism Mrs. Transome had no impulse to say one thing rather than another; as in a man who has just been branded on the forehead all wonted motives would be uprooted. Harold, on his side, had no wish opposed to filial kindness, but his busy thoughts were imperiously determined by habits which had no reference to any woman's feelings. . . ."

Radical, and, at home, supersedes her authority, her *raison d'être;* he terrifies her by proposing to follow up his suspicions concerning Matthew Jermyn's custodianship of the family interests. The mine waiting to be detonated will blast them all three. For Harold is also Jermyn's son.

It is remarkable—and it is characteristic of George Eliot's mature art—that the treatment of Mrs. Transome's early lapse should have in it nothing of the Victorian moralist. In the world of this art the atmosphere of the taboo is unknown; there is none of the excited hush, the skirting round, the thrill of shocked reprobation, or any of the forms of sentimentality typical of Victorian fiction when such themes are handled. There is instead an intently matter-of-fact directness: this is human nature, this is the fact and these are the inexorable consequences. Apart from the fear, the worst face, as Mrs. Transome sees it, of regret for the past is what we have here (it follows on the first long quotation made above from *Felix Holt*):

"In this position, with a great dread hanging over her, which Jermyn knew, and ought to have felt that he had caused her, she was inclined to lash him with indignation, to scorch him with the words that were just the fit names for his doings—inclined all the more when he spoke with an insolent blandness, ignoring all that was truly in her heart. But no sooner did the words 'You have brought it on me' rise within her than she heard within also the retort, 'You brought it on yourself.' Not for all the world beside could she bear to hear that retort uttered from without. What did she do? With strange sequence to all that rapid tumult, after a few moments' silence she said, in a gentle and almost tremulous voice—

"'Let me take your arm. . . .'

"As she took away her hand, Jermyn let his arm fall, put both his hands in his pockets, and shrugging his shoulders said, 'I shall use him as he uses me.'

"Jermyn had turned round his savage side, and the blandness was out of sight. It was this that had always frightened Mrs. Transome: there was a possibility of fierce insolence in this man who was to pass with those nearest to her as her indebted servant, but whose brand she secretly bore.

She was as powerless with him as she was with her son.

"This woman, who loved rule, dared not speak another word of attempted persuasion."

Mrs. Transome has, and can have, no impulse towards what the moralist means by repentance:

"She had no ultimate analysis of things that went beyond blood and family—the Herons of Fenshore or the Badgers of Hillbury. She had never seen behind the canvas with which her life was hung. In the dim background there was the burning mount and the tables of the law; in the foreground there was Lady Debarry privately gossiping about her, and Lady Wyvern finally deciding not to send her invitations to dinner."

She is herself here in her reaction to Jermyn's suggestion that he shall be saved by her telling Harold:

"'But now you have asked me, I will never tell him! Be ruined—no—do something more dastardly to save yourself. If I sinned, my judgment went beforehand—that I should sin for a man like you.'"

This limitation is of the essence of her tragedy; it goes, as George Eliot presents her, with her being an impressive and sympathy-commanding figure. Here we have her enduring the agonized helplessness of a moment of tension:

"When Harold left the table she went into the long drawing-room, where she might relieve her restlessness by walking up and down, and catch the sound of Jermyn's entrance into Harold's room, which was close by. Here she moved to and fro amongst the rose-coloured satin of chairs and curtains—the great story of this world reduced for her to the little tale of her own existence—dull obscurity everywhere, except where the keen light fell on the narrow track of her own lot, wide only for a woman's anguish. At last she heard the expected ring and footstep, and the opening and closing door. Unable to walk about any longer, she sank into a large cushioned chair, helpless and prayerless. She was not thinking of God's anger or mercy but of her son's. She was thinking of what might be brought, not by death, but by life."

There is no touch of the homiletic about this; it is dramatic constatation, poignant and utterly convincing, and the implied moral, which is a matter of the enacted inevitability, is that perceived by a psychological realist. As the strain develops for her, our sympathetic interest is painfully engaged, so that when we come to the critical point (Chapter XLII) at which Jermyn says, "It is not to be supposed that Harold would go against me . . . if he knew the whole truth," we feel the full atrocity the proposition has for her. Further, we take the full force and finality of the disaster represented by her now breaking her life-long resolve never to quarrel "with this man—never tell him what she knew him to be."

The man is perfectly done. For him Nemesis has a face corresponding to his moral quality; it is something he contemplates "in anger, in exasperation, that Harold, precisely Harold Transome, should have turned out to be the probable instrument of a visitation that would be bad luck, not justice; for is there any justice when ninety-nine men out of a hundred escape? He found himself beginning to hate Harold. . . ." By delicate touches the resemblance between father and son is conveyed to us, and the discrimination made between their respective egoisms.

If we agree that the two men are "women's men," it is not in any sense that detracts from their convincingness; it is rather in the sense that the penetrating and "placing" analysis of their masculinity is something, we feel, that it took a woman to do. Jermyn's case is Tito Melema's; this time not thought out in an effort to work from the abstract to the concrete, but presented in the life, with compelling reality; he is unquestionably "there" in the full concrete, and unquestionably (as Tito, in so far as he exists, is not) a man—one of "those who are led on through the years by the gradual demands of a selfishness which has spread its fibres far and wide through

the intricate vanities and sordid cares of an everyday existence."

As for Harold, he has "the energetic will, the quick perception, and the narrow imagination which make what is called the 'practical mind.' " He is a "clever, frank, good-natured egoist."

"His very good-nature was unsympathetic: it never came from any thorough understanding or deep respect for what was in the mind of the person he obliged or indulged; it was like his kindness to his mother—an arrangement of his for the happiness of others, which, if they were sensible, ought to succeed."

He cannot, of course, help his parentage; the ironic element of Nemesis in his disaster is given here:

" 'Confound the fellow—with his Mrs. Jermyn! Does he think we are on a footing for me to know anything about his wife?' "

It is characteristic of George Eliot that she can make such a man the focus of a profoundly moving tragedy: for Harold unquestionably becomes that for us at the point when, turning violently on Jermyn, who has been driven to come out with, "I am your father!" he catches sight, in the ensuing scuffle, of the two faces side by side in a mirror, and sees "the hated fatherhood reasserted." This may sound melodramatic as recapitulated here; that it should come with so final a rightness in the actual text shows with what triumphant success George Eliot has justified her high tragic conception of her theme. It is characteristic of her to be able to make a tragedy out of "moral mediocrity." The phrase is used to convey the redeemed Esther Lyon's sense of life at Transome Court, and Esther has been represented earlier as reflecting: "Mr. Transome had his beetles, but Mrs. Transome—?" There is nothing sentimental about George Eliot's vision of human mediocrity and "platitude," but she sees in them matters for compassion, and her dealings with them are assertions of human dignity. To be able to assert human dignity in this way is greatness: the contrast with Flaubert is worth pondering.

Felix Holt is not one of the novels that cultivated persons are supposed to have read, and, if read at all, it is hardly ever mentioned, so that there is reason for saying that one of the finest things in fiction is virtually unknown. It is exasperating that George Eliot should have embedded some of her maturest work in a mass that is so much other—though *Felix Holt* is not, like *Romola*, "unreadable," and the superlative quality of the live part ought to have compelled recognition. It is exasperating and it is, again, characteristic of her. Only one book can, as a whole (though not without qualification), be said to represent her mature genius. That, of course, is *Middlemarch*.

As for her rank among novelists, I take the challenge from a representative purveyor of currency, Oliver Elton: what he says we may confidently assume that thousands of the cultivated think it reasonable to say, and thousands of students in "Arts" courses are learning to say, either in direct study of him, or in the lecture-room. He says,[2] then, in discussing the "check to

[2] *A Survey of English Literature,* 1830–1880, Vol. II, Chapter XXIII. This chapter, "George Eliot and Anthony Trollope," is very representative of Elton—who is very representative of the academically esteemed "authority." It contains a convenient and unintentionally amusing conspectus of the ideas about George Eliot I have been combating. He exemplifies the gentleman's attitude towards Gwendolen: "The authoress drops on her a load of brickbats, and seems to wish to leave the impression that Gwendolen deserved them. She is young, and rather too hard, sprightly and rather domineering." (He says of *Middlemarch*: "This is almost one of the great novels of the language.")

George Eliot's reputation" given by the coming "into fuller view" of "two other masters of fiction"—Meredith and Hardy: "Each of these novelists saw the world of men and women more freely than George Eliot had done; and they brought into relief one of her greatest deficiencies, namely, that while exhaustively describing life, she is apt to miss the spirit of life itself." I can only say that this, for anyone whose critical education has begun, should be breath-taking in its absurdity, and affirm my conviction that, by the side of George Eliot—and the comparison shouldn't be necessary—Meredith appears as a shallow exhibitionist (his famous "intelligence" a laboured and vulgar brilliance) and Hardy, decent as he is, as a provincial manufacturer of gauche and heavy fictions that sometimes have corresponding virtues. For a positive indication of her place and quality I think of a Russian; not Turgenev, but a far greater, Tolstoy—who, we all know, is pre-eminent in getting "the spirit of life itself." George Eliot, of course, is not as transcendently great as Tolstoy, but she *is* great, and great in the same way. The extraordinary reality of *Anna Karenina* (his supreme masterpiece, I think) comes of an intense moral interest in human nature that provides the light and courage for a profound psychological analysis. This analysis is rendered in art (and *Anna Karenina,* pace Matthew Arnold, is wonderfully closely worked) by means that are like those used by George Eliot in *Gwendolen Harleth*—a proposition that will bear a great deal of considering in the presence of the text. Of George Eliot it can in turn be said that her best work has a Tolstoyan depth and reality.

emots say that Eliot does not deal with people's passion — since they don't come off.

V. S. Pritchett

George Eliot

She looked unusually charming today from the very fact that she was not vividly conscious of anything but of having a mind near her that asked her to be something better than she actually was.

IT IS easy to guess which of the mid-Victorian novelists wrote these lines. The use of the word "mind" for young man, the yearning for self-improvement in the heroine, and, lastly, the painful, reiterating English, all betray George Eliot. This description of Esther Lyon in *Felix Holt* might have been chipped out in stone for George Eliot's epitaph and, as we take down a novel of hers from the shelf, we feel we are about to lever off the heavy lid of some solid family tomb. Yet the epitaph is not hers alone. The unremitting ethic of self-improvement has been the sepulcher of all mid-Victorian fiction except *Wuthering Heights*. Today that ethic no longer claims the Esther Lyons of the English novel. The whole influence of psychology has turned our interest to what George Eliot would have called the downward path, to the failures of the will, the fulfillment of the heart, the vacillations of the sensibility, the perception of self-interest. We do not wish to be better than we are, but more fully what we are; and the wish is crossed by the vivid conflicts set up in our lives by the revolution that is going on in our society. The bottom has fallen out of our world and our Esthers are looking for a basis not for a ceiling to their lives.

But this does not mean that Esther Lyon is falsely drawn or that she is not a human being. Using our own jargon, all we have

a right to say is, that the objects of the super-ego have changed; and, in saying this, we should recall a minor point of importance. It is this. Not only English tradition from Fielding onwards, but no less a person than the author of the *Liaisons Dangereuses* delight in the delectable evasions of the prig and the reserve of the prude; and it would indeed be absurd to cut the aspirations to virtue out of characters and to leave only the virtue that is attained or is already there. The critic needs only to be clear about the kind of aspiration that is presented to him; and here we perceive that what separates us from Esther Lyon and her creator is a matter of history. She is impelled by the competitive reforming ethic of an expanding society. One might generalize without great danger and say that in all the mid-Victorian novels the characters are either going up in the world, in which case they are good; or they are going down in the world, in which case they are bad. Whereas Goldsmith and Fielding revelled in the misadventures of the virtuous and in the vagaries of Fortune—that tutelary goddess of a society dominated by merchant-speculators —a novelist like George Eliot writes at a time when Fortune has been torn down, when the earned increment of industry (and not the accidental coup of the gambler) has taken Fortune's place; and when character is tested not by hazard but, like the funds, by a measurable tendency to rise and fall.

Once her ethic is seen as the driving force of George Eliot we cease to be intimidated by it, and she emerges, for all her lectures, as the most formidable of the

From *The Living Novel*, New York, ... Reprinted by permission.

Victorian novelists. We dismiss the late-Victorian reaction from her work; our fathers were bored by her because they were importuned by her mind; she was an idol with feet of clay and, what was worse, appeared to write with them. But it is precisely because she was a mind and because she was a good deal of the schoolmistress that she interests us now. Where the other Victorian novelists seem shapeless, confused and without direction, because of their melodramatic plots and subplots and the careless and rich diversity of their characters, George Eliot marks out an ordered world, and enunciates a constructed judgment. If we read a novel in order to clarify our minds about human character, in order to pass judgment on the effect of character on the world outside itself, and to estimate the ideas people have lived by, then George Eliot is one of the first to give such an intellectual direction to the English novel. She is the first of the simplifiers, one of the first to cut moral paths through the picturesque maze of human motive. It is the intimidating role of the schoolmistress. And yet when we read a few pages of any of her books now, we notice less the oppression of her lectures and more the spaciousness of her method, the undeterred illumination which her habit of mind brings to human nature. We pass from the romantic shadows into an explicit, a prosaic but a relieving light.

Two of George Eliot's novels, it seems to me, will have a permanent place in English literature. As time goes by *Adam Bede* looks like our supreme novel of pastoral life; and I cannot see any novel of the nineteenth century that surpasses *Middlemarch* in range or construction. With *Adam Bede*, it is true, the modern reader experiences certain unconquerable irritations. We are faced by a sexual theme, and the Victorians were constitutionally unable to write about sexual love. In saying this we must agree that no English writer since the eighteenth century has been happy in this theme, for since that time we have lost

our regard for the natural man and the equanimity required for writing about him. The most we have a right to say about the Victorians is that, like the ingenious people who bricked up the windows of their houses and painted false ones on the wall, in order to escape the window tax, the Victorian novelists always chose to brick up the bedroom first.

Now in *Adam Bede* we are shocked by two things: the treatment of Hetty Sorrel and the marriage of Dinah and Adam at the end. It is clear that George Eliot's attitude to Hetty is a false one. The drawing of Hetty is neither observation from life nor a true recasting of experience by the imagination; it is a personal fantasy of George Eliot's. George Eliot was punishing herself and Hetty has to suffer for the "sins" George Eliot had committed, and for which, to her perhaps unconscious dismay, she herself was never punished. We rebel against the black and white view of life and when we compare *Adam Bede* with Scott's *Heart of Midlothian*, to which the former confessedly owes something of its plot, we are depressed by the decline of humanity that has set in since the eighteenth century. Humanity has become humanitarianism, uplift and, in the end, downright cruelty. The second quarrel we have with this book arises, as I have said, from the marriage of Adam and Dinah. There is no reason why a man who has suffered at the hands of a bad woman should not be rewarded and win the consolations of a good woman. If Adam Bede likes sermons, we say, better than infidelity let him have them: we all choose our own form of suffering. But George Eliot told lies about this marriage; or rather, she omitted a vital element from it. She left out the element of sexual jealousy or if she did not leave it out, she did not recognize it, because she cannot admit natural passions in a virtuous character. In that scene where Hetty pushes Dinah away from her in her bedroom, where Hetty is dressing up and dreaming her Bovary-like dreams, the reader sees something that George Eliot appears not to see. He is supposed to see that Hetty is self-willed; and this may be true, but he sees as well that Hetty's instincts have warned her of her ultimate rival. The failure to record jealousy and the attempt to transmute it so that it becomes the ambiguous if lofty repugnance to sin, springs from the deeper failure to face the nature of sexual passion.

This failure not only mars George Eliot's moral judgment but also represses her power as a story-teller. When Adam comes to Arthur Donnithorne's room at the Hermitage, Arthur stuffs Hetty's neckerchief into the wastepaper basket out of Adam's sight. The piece of silk is a powerful symbol. The reader's eye does not leave it. He waits for it to be found. But no, it simply lies there; its function is, as it were, to preach the risks of sin to the reader. Whereas in fact it ought to be made to disclose the inflammatory fact that the physical seduction took place in this very room. George Eliot refuses to make such a blatant disclosure not for æsthetic reasons, but for reasons of Victorian convention; and the result is that we have no real reason for believing Hetty *has* been seduced. Her baby appears inexplicably. The account of Hetty's flight is remarkable—it is far, far better than the corresponding episode in *The Heart of Midlothian*—but the whole business of the seduction and crime, from Adam's fight with Arthur Donnithorne in the woods to Hetty's journey to the scaffold, seems scarcely more than hearsay to the reader. And the reprieve of Hetty at the gallows adds a final unreality to the plot. It must also be said—a final cruelty.

Yet, such is George Eliot's quality as a novelist, none of these criticisms has any great importance. Like the tragedies of Hardy, *Adam Bede* is animated by the majestic sense of destiny which is fitting to novels of work and the soil. Majestic is perhaps the wrong word. George Eliot's sense of destiny was prosaic, not majestic; prosaic in the sense of unpoetical. One must judge a novel on its own terms; and from the beginning, in the lovely account of Dinah's preaching on the village green, George Eliot sets out the pieties which will enclose the drama that is to follow. Her handling of the Methodists and their faith is one of the memorable religious performances of English literature, for she neither adjures us nor satirizes them, but leaves a faithful and limpid picture of commonplace religion as a part of life. When she wrote of the peasants, the craftsmen, the yeomen, the clergy and squires of Warwickshire, George Eliot was writing out of childhood, from that part of her life which never betrayed her or any of the Victorians. The untutored sermons of Dinah have the same pastoral quality as the poutings of Hetty at the butter churn, the harangues of Mrs. Poyser at her cooking, or the remonstrances of Adam Bede at his carpenter's bench. In the mid-Victorian England of the railway and the drift to the towns, George Eliot was harking back to the last of the yeomen, among whom she was born and who brought out the warmth, the humor, the strength of her nature. We seem to be looking at one of Morland's pictures, at any of those domestic or rustic paintings of the Dutch school, where every leaf on the elm trees or the limes is painted, every gnarl of the bark inscribed, every rut followed with fidelity. We follow the people out of the hedgerows and the lanes into the kitchen. We see the endless meals, the eternal cup of tea; and the dog rests his head on our boot or flies barking to the yard, while young children toddle in and out of the drama at the least convenient moments. . . .

I doubt if any Victorian novelist has as much to teach the modern novelists as George Eliot; for although the English novel was established and became a constructed judgment on situations and people after she had written, it did not emulate her peasant sense of law. Hardy alone is her nearest parallel, but he differed from

V. S. Pritchett

her in conceiving a fate outside the will of man and indifferent to him. And her picture of country life is really closer to the country we know than Hardy's is, because he leaves us little notion of what the components of country society are. The English peasant lived and still lives in a milder, flatter world than Hardy's; a world where conscience and self-interest keep down the passions, like a pair of gamekeepers. It is true that George Eliot is cut off from the Rabelaisian malice and merriment of the country; she hears the men talk as they talk in their homes, not as they talk in the public-houses and the barns. But behind the salty paganism of country life stands the daily haggle of what people "ought" and "didn't ought" to do; the ancient nagging of church and chapel. All this is a minor matter beside her main lesson. What the great school-mistress teaches is the interest of massive writing, of placing people, of showing how even the minds of characters must be placed among other minds.

When we turn from *Adam Bede* to *Middlemarch* we find a novel in which her virtues as a novelist are established and assured; and where there is no sexual question to bedevil her judgment. No Victorian novel approaches *Middlemarch* in its width of reference, its intellectual power, or the imperturbable spaciousness of its narrative. It is sometimes argued by critics of contemporary literature that a return to Christianity is indispensable if we are to produce novels of the Victorian scale and authority, or indeed novels of any quality at all; but there are the novels of unbelievers like George Eliot and Hardy to discountenance them. The fact is that a wide and single purpose in the mind is the chief requirement outside of talent; a strong belief, a strong unbelief, even a strong egoism will produce works of the first order. If she had any religious leanings, George Eliot moved toward Judaism because of its stress on law; and if we think this preference purely intellectual and regard worry, that profoundly English

habit of mind, as her philosophy, the point is that it was strong, serious, comprehensive worry. A forerunner of the psychologists, she promises no heaven and threatens no hell; the best and the worst we shall get is Warwickshire. Her world is the world of will, the smithy of character, a place of knowledge and judgments. So, in the sense of worldly wisdom, is Miss Austen's. But what a difference there is. To repeat our earlier definition, if Miss Austen is the novelist of the ego and its platitudes, George Eliot is the novelist of the idolatries of the super-ego. We find in a book like *Middlemarch*, not character modified by circumstance only, but character first impelled and then modified by the beliefs, the ambitions, the spiritual objects which it assimilates. Lydgate's schemes for medical reform and his place in medical science are as much part of his character as his way with the ladies. And George Eliot read up her medical history in order to get his position exactly right. Dorothea's yearning for a higher life of greater usefulness to mankind will stay with her all her days and will make her a remarkable but exasperating woman; a fool for all her cleverness. George Eliot gives equal weight to these important qualifications. Many Victorian novelists have lectured us on the careers and aspirations of their people; none, before George Eliot, showed us the unity of intellect, aspiration and nature in action. Her judgment on Lydgate as a doctor is a judgment on his fate as a man:

He carried to his studies in London, Edinburgh and Paris the conviction that the medical profession as it might be was the finest in the world; presenting the most perfect interchange between science and art; offering the most direct alliance between intellectual conquest and the social good. Lydgate's nature demanded this combination: he was an emotional creature, with a flesh and blood sense of fellowship, which withstood all the abstractions of special study. He cared not only for "Cases," but for John and Elizabeth, especially Elizabeth.

60   Discussions of George Eliot

The Elizabeth, who was not indeed to wreck Lydgate's life, but (with far more probability) to corrupt his ideals and turn him into the smart practitioner, was Rosamund, his wife. Yet, in its own way, Rosamund's super-ego had the most distinguished ideals. A provincial manufacturer's daughter, she too longed idealistically to rise; the desire was not vulgar until she supposed that freedom from crude middle-class notions of taste and bearing could only be obtained by marriage to the cousin of a baronet; and was not immoral until she made her husband's conscience pay for her ambitions. The fountain, George Eliot is always telling us, cannot rise higher than its source.

Such analyses of character have become commonplace to us. When one compares the respectable Rosamund Lydgate with, say, Becky Sharp, one sees that Rosamund is not unique. Where *Middlemarch* is unique in its time is in George Eliot's power of generalization. The last thing one accuses her of is unthinking acceptance of convention. She seeks, in her morality, the positive foundation of natural law, a kind of Fate whose measures are as fundamental as the changes of the seasons in nature. Her intellect is sculptural. The clumsiness of style does not denote muddle, but an attempt to carve decisively. We feel the clarifying force of a powerful mind. Perhaps it is not naturally powerful. The power may have been acquired. There are two George Eliots: the mature, experienced, quiet-humored Midlander who wrote the childhood pages of *The Mill on the Floss;* and the naïve, earnest and masterly intellectual with her half-dozen languages and her scholarship. But unlike the irony of our time, hers is at the expense not of belief, but of people. Behind them, awful but inescapable to the eye of conscience, loom the statues of what they ought to have been. Hers is a mind that has grown by making judgments—as Mr. Gladstone's head was said to have grown by making speeches.

Middlemarch resumes the observation and experience of a lifetime. Until this book George Eliot often strains after things beyond her capacity, as Dorothea Casaubon strained after a spiritual power beyond her nature. But now in *Middlemarch* the novelist is reconciled to her experience. In Dr. Casaubon George Eliot sees that tragedy may paralyze the very intellect which was to be Dorothea's emancipation. Much of herself (George Eliot said, when she was accused of portraying Mark Pattison) went into Casaubon, and I can think of no other English novel before or since which has so truthfully, so sympathetically and so intimately described the befogged and grandiose humiliations of the scholar, as he turns at bay before the vengeance of life. Casaubon's jealousy is unforgettable, because, poisonous though it is, it is not the screech of an elderly cuckold, but the voice of strangled nature calling for justice. And notice, here, something very characteristic; George Eliot's pity flows from her moral sense, from the very seat of justice, and not from a sentimental heart.

Middlemarch is the first of many novels about groups of people in provincial towns. They are differentiated from each other not by class or fortune only, but by their moral history, and this moral differentiation is not casual, it is planned and has its own inner hierarchy. Look at the groups. Dorothea, Casaubon and Ladislaw seek to enter the highest spiritual fields—not perhaps the highest, for us, because, as we have seen, the world of George Eliot's imagination was prosaic and not poetic—still, they desire, in their several ways, to influence the standards of mankind. There is Lydgate, who is devoted to science and expects to be rewarded by a career. He and his wife are practical people, who seek power. The pharisaical Bulstrode, the banker, expects to rise both spiritually and financially at once, until he sits on the right hand of God, the Father; a businessman with a bad conscience, he is the father of the Buchmanites and of all success-religions. The Garths, being country people

V. S. Pritchett

and outside all this urban world, believe simply in the virtue of work as a natural law and they are brought up against Fred Vincy, Rosamund's brother. He, as a horsey young man educated beyond his means, has a cheerful belief in irresponsible Style and in himself as a thing of pure male beauty with a riding crop. We may not accept George Eliot's standards, but we can see that they are not conventional, and that they do not make her one-sided. She is most intimately sympathetic to human beings and is never sloppy about them. When Vincy quarrels with Bulstrode about Fred's debts, when Casaubon's jealousy of Ladislaw secretes its first venom, when Lydgate tries vainly to talk about money to his wife or Fred goes to his mad old grandfather for a loan, vital human issues are raised. The great scenes of *Middlemarch* are exquisite, living transpositions of real moral dilemmas. Questions of principle are questions of battle; they point the weapons of the human comedy, and battle is not dull. In consequence, George Eliot's beliefs are rarely boring, because they are a dynamism. They correspond to psychological and social realities, though more especially (on the large scale) to the functions of the will; they are boring only when, in the Victorian habit, she harangues the reader and pads out the book with brainy essays.

I see I have been writing about *Middlemarch* as though it was a piece of engineering. What about the life, the humor, the pleasure? There are failures: Dorothea and Ladislaw do not escape the fate of so many Victorian heroes and heroines who are frozen by their creator's high-mindedness. Has George Eliot forgotten how much these two difficult, sensitive and proud people will annoy each other by the stupidity which so frequently afflicts the intellectual? Such scruples, such playing-acting! But Lydgate and Rosamund quarreling about money; Rosamund quietly thwarting her husband's decisions, passing without conscience to love affairs with his friends and ending as a case-hardened widow who efficiently finds a second father for her family—these things are perfect. Mary Garth defying the old miser is admirable. But the most moving thing in the book— and I always think this is the real test of a novelist—is given to the least likeable people. Bulstrode's moral ruin, and his inability to confess to his dull wife, is portrayed in a picture of dumb human despondency which recalls a painting by Sickert. One hears the clock tick in the silence that attends the wearing down of two lives that can cling together but dare not speak. . . .

There is no real madness in George Eliot. Both heavy feet are on the ground. Outside of *Wuthering Heights* there is no madness in Victorian fiction. The Victorians were a histrionic people who measured themselves by the Elizabethans; and George Eliot, like Browning and Tennyson, was compared to Shakespeare by her contemporaries. The comparison failed, if only because madness is lacking. Hysteria, the effect of the exorbitant straining of their wills, the Victorians did, alas, too often achieve. George Eliot somehow escapes it. She is too levelheaded. One pictures her, in life, moralizing instead of making a scene. There is no hysteria in *Middlemarch;* perhaps there are no depths because there is so much determination. But there is a humane breadth and resolution in this novel which offers neither hope nor despair to mankind but simply the necessity of fashioning a moral life. George Eliot's last words on her deathbed might, one irreverently feels, be placed on the title-page of her collected works: "Tell them," she is reported to have said, "the pain is on the left side." Informative to the last and knowing better than the doctor, the self-made positivist dies.

Joan Bennett

Vision and Design

WHEN we read George Eliot's novels for the first time we are likely to be too much absorbed in the unfolding of the story to be conscious of any peculiar characteristics of her vision of life or her method of presenting it. Like most of the great Victorian novelists, she has the spell-binding power of the Ancient Mariner; we are forced to attend, the world in which her characters move becomes the real world, unquestioningly accepted. The principal characters take their place in the foreground, our sympathies are firmly engaged for them and we are carried forward by that curiosity which novel readers share with children, the desire to know what happens next. Only when the book is closed and we cease to participate in the life of Hayslope, St Ogg's or Middlemarch can we begin to inquire what makes up the characteristic impression of a George Eliot novel; by then the spell is broken. But it is well to remember that her books are great works of fiction, partly because they have this magic; no analysis can reproduce it any more than an analysis of a poem can reproduce the effect of poetry. With fiction as with poetry the first necessity (if the work is to become an effective part of our experience) is to submit to the spell: intellectual appreciation and evaluation follow after. It is, of course, the story, not the mere plot, that works the spell. The plot is preconceived by the author and can be summarized by the critic, but the stories, George Eliot herself tells us, "grow in me like plants." It is the growth of the plant, the gradual unfolding of character in its environment, that

compels attention, not the mere concatenation of events. The story-teller works her will on us because we are convinced that these people and this town or village exist. The novels, like any other stories that beguile us, provide us the pleasure of disinterested sympathy. When we read of the sufferings of fictitious, or, for that matter, of historical characters, we can indulge in the natural human tendency to sympathize without any possibility of being required to act. In so far as an unimaginative hardness of heart is normal, it is probably the result of unconscious self-protection against such a demand, and the satisfaction following upon reading a fiction or witnessing a drama suggests that, when there is a need to be on the defensive, we enjoy being made to understand our fellow-sufferers. The ultimate value of such aesthetic experience will depend upon how far the pleasurable exercise—playing at sympathy—can affect our conduct in the workaday world. The immediate effect of reading George Eliot's novels is, then, one which her works have in common with all successful fiction, it is hard to put the book down. Jane Carlyle read the *Scenes of Clerical Life* sitting up in bed with a high temperature and a sore throat, and wrote to the unknown author:

> You will believe me that the book needed to be something more than a "new novel" for me; that I *could* at my years, and after so much reading, read it in positive torment, and be beguiled by it of the torment.[1]

[1] J. W. Cross, *George Eliot's Life, Letters and Journals*, vol. II, p. 10.

From *George Eliot, Her Mind and Her Art,* Cambridge University Press, 1948. Reprinted by permission of the publisher.

Joan Bennett

That power to beguile persisted and increased (with partial lapses in *Romola* and *Daniel Deronda*) and it is only when we shake ourselves free from the beguilement that we notice that the vision of life we have shared has its individual character. Despite all the differences between George Eliot's novels, certain broad resemblances mark them as products of a single mind.

There is, first of all, a resemblance in the way she shapes her novels and consequently in the total impression any one of them leaves with the reader. When we try, after an interval, to recall any one of them we find ourselves thinking as much about the life of a village or a provincial town, or of the interrelation of groups of families, as about the central drama. George Eliot herself said, with reference to *Romola*: "It is the habit of my imagination to strive after as full a vision of the medium in which a character moves as of the character itself," and that habit accounts for the depth and breadth of the vision of life she communicates. As a matter of fact the word "strive," appropriate to *Romola* where the "medium" was fifteenth-century Florence whose habits of life and thought she had to reconstruct on a basis of research, is misleading when applied to her English novels. The rural and provincial life of England she had known from childhood: her imagination contained it rather than strove after it. But it is clear that she gave as much attention to presenting the outer circle of her design as the inner. The outer circle within which the dramatic situation is contained, is an organic human society and her novels are deeply imbued with the spirit of a particular place and time.

Adam Bede is the earliest and simplest example of the typical George Eliot form. The life of Hayslope envelops the tragedy. We come to know all grades of its society, artisans, labourers, farmers, rector, schoolmaster, innkeeper and squire. It is an active community in which most men or women have work to do and their character is affected by that work. That character is also the product of religious influences; we become aware of the impact of Methodism upon the inhabitants of Hayslope and of the more subtly pervasive influence of traditional Anglicanism. In the Third Book the whole community is assembled at Donnithorne Chase to celebrate the young squire's coming of age; by that time the pattern of living out of which the central characters emerge is clearly established and their drama is already under way. After the climax, when Hetty Sorrel has been condemned to death, reprieved and deported and another author would feel that the work was complete, there is a Sixth Book, balancing the Third. In it the rhythm of Hayslope life is re-established and, with the inevitable gaps made by the intervening event, a Harvest supper reassembles the same community as celebrated the young squire's birthday. The central tragedy is intimately connected with this background. The full effect of Arthur Donnithorne's yielding to the sensuous appeal of the pretty child-like Hetty and of all that ensues depends upon the relation of both characters to their world. The pride and well-grounded self-respect of the Poysers, established in the reader's mind by the vivid pictures of their surroundings, their working day, their home life, their Sunday observance, and the neighbours' opinion of them, all play their part in causing the tragedy and in heightening the bitterness of its effect. It is the social background the Poysers have provided for their niece and the standard of conduct imbibed from it that make it inevitable for Hetty to take flight before the birth of her baby; it is the esteem in which they are held by which the reader measures their shame and it is the clear sense he acquires of their identification with Hayslope by which he measures the anguish as well as the probability of their contemplated uprooting when the shame is known to them. Similarly, it is Arthur's upbringing, his

64 Discussions of George Eliot

relations with his grandfather, the squire, his high conception of the love and esteem he will earn from all his dependents when he inherits the land, that define the price he pays for his weakness. There is no part of what we have learnt of the outer circle that does not affect our sense of the inner. The cultured benignity of the rector, the moral enthusiasm of the Methodists, the simple ignorance of the country-folk, all make their own impact on the central characters and help to determine the events. Although the impression while we read is of a leisurely sequence of naturalistic scenes of comedy or of pathos and of a world richly populated with entertaining characters, when we look back we find that every individual scene or character is directly or indirectly related to the simple story at the core of the book, of the carpenter's betrothed betrayed by the squire's grandson. In its setting this common-place story becomes widely significant. The simple, well-contrived pattern conveys the sense of a social structure enclosing four human beings as completely as the soil encloses the roots of a growing plant and, in so doing, it illustrates one aspect of the author's vision of life.

Although the formal pattern is not elsewhere so simple and symmetrical as it is in *Adam Bede*—where the assembly of the villagers on the green to hear the preaching in Book I, their assembly at the birthday feast in Book III and at the Harvest supper in Book VI provide rests that divide the composition into almost equal parts— the general character of the design, an individual tragedy surrounded by the life of the community, is similar in all George Eliot's novels, except *Daniel Deronda*, where the absence of such an enclosing community is an important part of her conception. In her own view the lack of symmetry in *The Mill on the Floss* was responsible for her imperfect fulfilment of her intention, and for the dissatisfaction that most readers feel about the end of that novel:

. . . the tragedy is not adequately prepared. This is a defect which I felt while writing the third volume, and have felt ever since the MS. left me. The *Epische Breite* into which I was beguiled by love of my subject in the first two volumes, caused a want of proportionate fullness in the treatment of the third, which I shall always regret.[2]

The regret is justified in so far as the compression of the Maggie and Stephen episode contributes to its faulty presentation. Yet the epic breadth of the first two volumes is warranted by the completeness with which we come to understand the pressure of her surroundings on Maggie's developing personality which will, in turn, condition the central drama. We are brought to a full realization of those surroundings because, in a series of scenes, each with their own intrinsic value as social comedy, or drama, we grow familiar with a number of households and their way of life, which is both individual and representative. There is, for instance, the financially precarious home life of the Tullivers themselves; Mr Tulliver speculative, perplexed and, compared with his wife, adventurous, and Mrs Tulliver, foolish and faithful, torn between loyalty to her own family and to the proud conventions of her Dodson upbringing. Then there are the prosperous middle-class homes of her sisters; Mrs Glegg's home at St Ogg's with its "front and back parlours so that she had two points of view from which she could observe the weakness of her fellow-beings, and reinforce her thankfulness for her own exceptional strength of mind," and the elegant home of Mrs Pullet with its "front door mats by no means intended to wipe shoes on: the very scraper had a deputy to do its dirty work"; and we are shown the well-conducted home life of Tom's ambitious clerical tutor, or, in contrast to all these, the home of Mr Tulliver's sister, Aunt Moss,

[2] Cross, vol. II, p. 262; from a letter to Blackwood replying to the criticism of Sir Edward Bulwer Lytton.

who struggles to feed and clothe a large family on the proceeds of a farm starved of capital, since she had committed the indiscretion of marrying solely for love. All these aspects of life that the reader encounters as they impinge on Maggie's childhood, and that he relishes for their own vivid humour or pathos, convey the breadth of the world that surrounds an individual life and the narrowness of the space in which such a life can freely grow.

The difference in quality between George Eliot's novels is closely related to the degree of success with which she gives life to the social world surrounding her central characters. In her first period, from the *Scenes of Clerical Life* to *Silas Marner*, she plants those characters in the environment with which she had been familiar since her childhood, and, for many readers, it is these novels that give the most delight. Certainly in them her characteristic humour, compounded of compassion, a sense of the incongruous, and an ear for dialogue that is both racy and individual, has the freest play. But when she returned, in *Middlemarch*, with a more assured command of her art, to the environment she most fully understood, she achieved her masterpiece. It is true that this great novel lacks some of the qualities of the first period; it has less spontaneous gaiety, partly because the provincial town gave her less scope for comedy than did the rural environment. There is also an aspect of her genius, absent here, which is more often found in the poet than in the prose artist, an ability to simplify without distorting human truths, so that they can be presented symbolically as they are in the legend of *Silas Marner*. The impulse towards such simplification is intrusive at the close of *The Mill on the Floss,* where the reunion in death of Maggie and Tom is out of key with the rest of the work, and a similar discord between two modes of treatment distorts *Daniel Deronda*. But in *Silas Marner* the naturalistic treatment and the legendary story are happily com-bined and produce a minor masterpiece. Nevertheless, though certain excellencies must be sought elsewhere, *Middlemarch* is her widest and deepest study of the inter-penetration between the life of a community and the individual lives that compose it.

The relative failure of *Romola, Felix Holt* and *Daniel Deronda* is partly due to the fact that in these three works, for different reasons, the social background is imperfectly focussed. In *Romola* this is the result of transplanting her scene to a world that she needed to reconstruct with laborious intellectual effort. In *Felix Holt*, although the ingredients of a first-rate George Eliot novel are all there, they are not successfully integrated. The romance of Esther and Felix usurps the foreground of the book and the more serious and interesting study of Mrs Transome and Jermyn, her son's father, is relegated to the background. The reader's interest oscillates between the political theme—the two contrasted radicals and their relations to the new voter—and the moral theme, illustrated by Mrs Transome reaping the fruits of her former self-indulgence and Esther moving towards her self-abnegating choice of true love and modest means. Because the various threads of interest do not compose into a single pattern *Felix Holt*, though enjoyable, does not enlarge the field of understanding as do the major novels. The social environment is not sufficiently convincing to provide a unifying centre; whereas, in the vintage works, the community has an identity as recognizable and persuasive as that of the central characters.

The case of *Daniel Deronda* is different. In this book the absence of an enveloping society for either Gwendolen or Daniel is a part of the author's central conception. Both characters are incomplete because they have been deprived of such a soil in which to grow. Gwendolen's selfishness and narrowness of vision and Daniel's quest for some communal tie to direct his altruistic aspirations are the outcome of a lack, in the early life of each, of just such a

66 Discussions of George Eliot

background as Hayslope provided for the characters in *Adam Bede,* the Dodson-Tulliver world for Maggie, or Middlemarch for Dorothea. George Eliot's perception of the dependence of human beings on one another and on their social and religious traditions is as keen in *Daniel Deronda* as elsewhere, but she attempts here to embody it by a process the reverse of the one she had mastered. Hitherto in her books the central drama had sprung from a tension between the individual and the community; she had posed her characters with the problem of adapting their personal desires, noble or selfish, to the inescapable surrounding conditions represented by an organic society. Her most characteristic gift was her power to embody those conditions and to frame her story within them. But in *Daniel Deronda* the social scenes, often vividly presented (for instance, the gambling scene; or the family life of the Cohens; or the archery party), are essentially disparate. They are of no service in fusing the themes into a single whole. Some incoherence in this last novel is due to the fact that the new approach presented a new problem in composition which was not successfully solved. The characteristic form of her novels is the product of a vision of life the source of which lay far back in her childhood. When she had found herself unable to accept the Christian dogmas she held fast to the ethical beliefs of which those dogmas had been the embodiment. She doubted the factual truth of the miraculous story told in the Gospels, and she doubted the factual truth of the theological dogma elicited from that story and developed in the tradition of the Church; but she had no doubt that human happiness and the full development of individual personality depend on mutual love and service. In 1848, eight years before she herself began to write fiction, and six years before she made her own moral choice to live with Lewes in defiance of the laws, conventions and religious teachings of the community, she commented on

Charlotte Brontë's treatment of Jane Eyre's problem:

All self-sacrifice is good, but one would like it to be in a somewhat nobler cause than that of a diabolical law which chains a man soul and body to a putrefying carcase.[3]

The statement occurs in a letter to Charles Bray; the first clause, implying that self-sacrifice is good in itself, would certainly have been modified later and might even then have been otherwise expressed if she had been writing more carefully than intimate correspondence requires. The conception of the good in self-sacrifice embodied in the novels is that it is relative and not absolute. Self-sacrifice is good because human happiness depends on it; man cannot live alone and social life is incompatible with unrestrained self-indulgence. This truth was most fully understood by her in relation to the English village and small town community life in which she had been bred, and in such communities, impregnated with social and religious traditions emerging in the conventions and observances of family and social life, it could be clearly illustrated. The problems which face Hetty and Arthur, Maggie and Stephen, Godfrey and Silas, Lydgate and Dorothea, are all problems concerned with the adjustment of the individual to the community, and with the discovery of a mean point between complete self-repression and unchecked self-indulgence. The motive for self-sacrifice is the happiness of other people and George Eliot composed her fictions in such a way as to set that motive in a clear light. But, by the time she wrote *Daniel Deronda,* she herself had long ceased to live in a community governed by traditions slowly evolved through centuries and unquestionably accepted by the majority. In the intellectual and artistic world in which she and George Henry Lewes were ultimately made welcome, there was no such tradition, woven of inherited beliefs, customs

[3] Cross, vol. I, p. 191.

and conventions. Before she wrote *Daniel Deronda* she must have begun to ask herself how the law of mutual service and mutual deference to opinion operates for the *déraciné*. The unsatisfactory invention of Daniel's discovery of a Jewish allegiance and a mission to his people is an attempt to answer that question for him. It is not an intellectually satisfactory answer; nor has she successfully solved the artistic problem of linking the rootlessness of Daniel with the differently derived rootlessness of Gwendolen. The relationship between the two characters is potentially interesting, but they are arbitrarily brought together. Moreover, Daniel remains the symbol of an idea, whereas Gwendolen is the product of creative insight. The relative failure of the last novel is, in part, the failure to find an adequate substitute for that portrayal of a total society which gives her best novels their distinctive form. . . .

The organic or living form of her novels, within the expected framework, is different from anything that had gone before. It resembles, in some respects, Jane Austen's form in so far as the central characters are deeply rooted in their social environment which determines their story as much as does their individual character. The difference is that the social environment is wider, more complex, made up of a greater variety of minor characters drawn from many more social and economic levels, and also that the display of this outer circle or environment is more conscious. Jane Austen took her social *milieu* for granted; its manners and traditions were, for her, as little open to question as the laws of na-

ture. George Eliot was aware of the ethical, religious and social conventions of the world she paints as a product of history, evolved in time and changing with time. She was consciously interested in the pressure all these exert on individual lives and and in the existence of a problem concerned with resisting or succumbing to that pressure. She shares the modern consciousness of man in a changing and developing society. Consequently, the organic form of her novels—an inner circle (a small group of individuals involved in a moral dilemma) surrounded by an outer circle (the social world within which the dilemma has to be resolved)—is more significant than in any preceding fiction. Furthermore, her perception of individual human beings is more complex than that of her predecessors. She never suggests a simple division of characters into good and bad. The individual, like the environment, has evolved and is evolving; his or her behaviour at any given moment is the inevitable result of all that has gone before; therefore, while the action can itself be judged, both in relation to its consequences and to its aesthetic beauty (an action that pleases or displeases), the doer is not presented judicially but compassionately. In her discourse George Eliot sometimes deviates from this attitude and her novel suffers accordingly. But whenever her reflective powers are in due subordination to her creative gift, wherever, as usually happens in the dialogue, she responds to her characters rather than thinks about them, the reader feels with them and the total effect of her novel is an increase of understanding and compassion.

Basil Willey

George Eliot

IN THE present book, which attempts to follow some of the main currents of thought and belief in nineteenth century England, George Eliot must needs occupy a central place. Probably no English writer of the time, and certainly no novelist, more fully epitomizes the century; her development is a paradigm, her intellectual biography a graph, of its most decided trend. Starting from evangelical Christianity, the curve passes through doubt to a reinterpreted Christ and a religion of humanity: beginning with God, it ends in Duty. George Eliot's representative quality is due largely to her unique position, amongst imaginative writers, as a focus for the best (and the worst) that was being said and thought in her time, in Europe as well as at home. No one was more thoroughly abreast of the newest thought, the latest French or German theory, the last interpretations of dogma, the most up-to-date results in anthropology, medicine, biology or sociology; it is she who first translates Strauss's *Life of Jesus* and Feuerbach's *Essence of Christianity;* if a Mackay writes *The Progress of the Intellect* (1850), it is Miss Evans who must review it for the *Westminster.* She was the first English writer to bring an intellect of that calibre to the service of fiction, and the wonder perhaps is that this preponderant cerebration did not devour her creative instinct more completely than it did. But as with Wordsworth, whom she greatly reverenced and in some ways resembled, the heart in her was kept alive by the recollection of her early life, and of the scenes and people associated with the feelings of childhood. In a sense her early

novels are her *Prelude,* that is, the means by which she pierced below the hard crust formed by the years of translating, reviewing and mental overforcing, to the quickening beds of heartfelt memory which lay beneath. Having achieved this recovery of time past, she was then able to see in truer perspective the relations between advancing intellect and backward-yearning affections. From the very outset, however, she showed the instinct—which was deeply imbedded in the consciousness of the century as a whole—to see both sides of any question: to tolerate the ordinary while admiring the ideal, to cling to the old while accepting the new, to retain the core of traditions while mentally criticizing their forms. She succeeded, better than J. S. Mill, in uniting what he described as the two main streams of the nineteenth century mind—its two kinds of one-sidedness—the Benthamite, which stands outside and tests all received opinions, and the Coleridgean, which tries from within to discover what is true in them. We see this action and reaction going on both in her own life and in the novels. From the latter let us here take two preliminary examples—the first, significantly enough, from the very opening of her first fiction:

"Shepperton Church was a very different looking building five-and-twenty years ago. To be sure, its substantial stone tower looks at you through its intelligent eye, the clock, with the friendly expression of former days; but in everything else what changes! Now there is a wide span of slated roof flanking the old steeple; the windows are tall and symmetrical, the outer doors are resplendent with oak-graining, the inner doors rev-

From *Nineteenth Century Studies,* London, Chatto and Windus, 1949. Reprinted by permission of the publisher.

erentially noiseless with a garment of red baize; and the walls, you are convinced, no lichen will ever again effect a settlement upon—they are smooth and innutrient as the summit of the Rev. Amos Barton's head, after ten years of baldness and supererogatory soap. Pass through the baize doors and you will see the nave filled with well-shaped benches, understood to be free seats; while in certain eligible corners, less directly under the fire of the clergyman's eye, there are pews reserved for the Shepperton gentility. Ample galleries are supported on iron pillars, and in one of them stands the crowning glory, the very clasp or aigrette of Shepperton church-adornment—namely, an organ, not very much out of repair, on which a collector of small rents, differentiated by the force of circumstances into an organist, will accompany the alacrity of your departure after the blessing, by a sacred minuet or an easy 'Gloria.'

"Immense improvement! says the well-regulated mind, which unintermittingly rejoices in the New Police, the Tithe Commutation Act, the penny post, and all guarantees of human advancement, and has no moments when conservative-reforming intellect does a little Toryism by the sly, revelling in regret that dear, old, brown, crumbling, picturesque inefficiency is everywhere giving place to spick-and-span new-painted, new-varnished efficiency, which will yield endless diagrams, plans, elevations, and sections, but alas! no picture. Mine, I fear, is not a well-regulated mind: it has an occasional tenderness for old abuses; it lingers with a certain fondness over the days of nasal clerks and top-booted parsons, and has a sigh for the departed shades of vulgar errors." [1]

The second illustration is from *The Mill on the Floss:*

"Very commonplace, even ugly, that furniture of our early home might look if it were put up to auction; an improved taste in upholstery scorns it; and is not the striving after something better and better in our surroundings, the grand characteristic that distinguishes man from the brute . . . ? But Heaven knows where that striving might lead us, if our affections had not a trick of twining round those old inferior things—if the loves and sanctities of our life had no deep immovable roots in memory." [2]

In what follows I hope to suggest that this "conservative-reforming" impulse was the leading *motif* of her life: that her lifelong quest, as it was Comte's and the century's, was for a reconcilement between these opposites, a synthesis (as Comte would say) between the Static and Dynamic principles, between Order and Progress, Tradition and Enlightenment, the heart and the head. . . .

Whoever has been reading George Eliot will recognize that with most of the underlying principles of Strauss, Comte and Feuerbach she was in agreement. The supersession of God by Humanity, of Faith by Love and Sympathy, the elimination of the supernatural, the elevation of the natural, the subordination of intellect to heart, thought to feeling—these may all be found in her novels as well as in her letters. Heaven will not help us, so we must help one another; this realization tinges our whole life with anguish, but it is the cross which the new elect must bear:

"The 'highest calling and election' is to *do without opium*, and live through all our pain with conscious, clear-eyed endurance." [3]

But her studies, as well as her own inmost propensities, inclined her to rely upon truth of feeling, and this engendered a wide tolerance and reverence for all religious forms which have expressed, and still express, the primary needs of the human heart. To her "conservative-reforming intellect," the merely negative kinds of "free-thinking" were hateful:

"I have a growing conviction," she writes to Sara Hennell, while at work on *Scenes of Clerical Life*, "that we may measure true moral and intellectual culture by the comprehension and veneration given to all forms of thought and feeling which have influenced large masses of mankind—and of all intolerance the intolerance calling itself philosophical is the most odious to me." [4]

[3] Cross, [*George Eliot's Life*,] vol. ii, p. 283 (letter to Mme Bodichon, Dec. 26, 1860).

[4] *Ibid.*, vol. i, p. 432 (Feb. 24, 1857).

[1] *Scenes of Clerical Life*, p. 1.

[2] Bk. ii, ch. i (p. 173 in World's Classics ed.)

Discussions of George Eliot

And again, to Charles Bray (July 5, 1859):

"people are, for the most part, so incapable of comprehending the state of mind which cares for that which is essentially human in all forms of belief, and desires to exhibit it under all forms with loving truthfulness. Freethinkers are scarcely wider than the orthodox in this matter,—they all want to see themselves and their own opinions held up as the true and the lovely." [5]

Lord David Cecil will have it that George Eliot was "not religious"; I cannot agree with him—or rather, I cannot agree that that is the least misleading way of saying what he means. "Religious" seems to me to be just what she was, and many others of whom she is the type; the whole predicament she represents was that of the religious temperament cut off by the *Zeitgeist* from the traditional objects of veneration, and the traditional intellectual formulations. [6] She was not, of course, a "practising Christian," but in her estrangement from the "religion *about* Jesus" she was none the further from the "religion *of* Jesus." She knew the hunger and thirst after righteousness, and the need for renunciation—the need to lose one's life in order to gain it. And, though her religious consciousness was pre-eminently moral, it was not exclusively so; she also had the faculty of reverence, the capacity to acknowledge the reality of the unseen. When reading Darwin's *Origin of Species* she writes:

"to me the Development Theory, and all other explanations of processes by which things came to be, produce a feeble impression compared with the mystery that lies under the processes." [7]

Hers was in fact the middle position of conservative-liberalism; it is a position not easy to sustain, and I do not think that George Eliot ever—at least not for any long period—recovered lasting heart's-ease. There could only be, for her, effort, striving, endurance, and that "terrible earnestness" recorded by F. W. H. Myers.

"I have faith in the working out of higher possibilities than the Catholic or any other Church has presented," she writes in Comtist language, "and those who have strength to wait and endure are bound to accept no formula which their whole souls—their intellect as well as their emotions—do not embrace with entire reverence."

—and then follows the phrase about *doing without opium*. [8] One of the clearest statements is this, taken from another letter to Mme Bodichon (written during the composition of *Romola*):

"Pray don't ever ask me again not to rob a man of his religious belief, as if you thought my mind tended to such robbery. I have too profound a conviction of the efficacy that lies in all sincere faith, and the spiritual blight that comes with no faith, to have any negative propagandism in me. In fact, I have very little sympathy with Freethinkers as a class, and have lost all interest in mere antagonism to religious doctrines. I care only to know, if possible, the lasting meaning that lies in all religious doctrine from the beginning till now." [9]

It is a sentiment which would have been echoed by Coleridge, Carlyle, Maurice, Arnold, Sidgwick and many others. Her technique for retaining what she considered this "lasting meaning," while rejecting what her intellect found unacceptable, was that of Strauss and the German "higher criticism," and of Matthew Arnold and later modernists. Writing of Renan's *Vie de Jésus* she says:

"It seems to me the soul of Christianity lies not at all in the facts of an individual life, but in the ideas of which that life was the meeting-point and the new starting-point. We can never have a satisfactory basis for the history of the man Jesus, but that negation does not affect the Idea of the Christ either in its historical influence or its great symbolic meanings." [10]

[5] *Ibid.*, vol. ii, p. 118.

[6] . . . Was Carlyle "not religious"?

[7] Cross, *op. cit.*, vol. ii, p. 148 (letter to Mme Bodichon, Dec. 5, 1859).

[8] *Ibid.*, vol. ii, p. 283.

[9] *Ibid.*, p. 343 (Nov. 26, 1862).

[10] *Ibid.*, pp. 359–60 (to Mrs Peter Taylor, July 30, 1863).

Basil Willey

Or again:

"The divine will is simply so much as we have ascertained of the facts of existence which compel obedience at our peril." [11]

. . . She would go to church constantly, she says, for the sake of fellowship in worshipping "the highest good," were there no reasons against following this inclination. For those without definite religious convictions, church-going will be better than mere negation. My last extracts on this theme are from letters written to Mrs Ponsonby in 1874 and 1875:

"My books have for their main bearing a conclusion . . . without which I could not have cared to write any representation of human life—namely, that the fellowship between man and man which has been the principle of development, social and moral, is not dependent on conceptions of what is not man: and that the idea of God, so far as it has been a high spiritual influence, is the ideal of a goodness entirely human (i.e. an exaltation of the human)."

Loss of belief in a future life, she goes on, does not rob us of our moral sense, our sense of duty, our sympathy; we retain our "sense of quality in actions," just as we continue to appreciate colour even after becoming aware of the laws of the spectrum. We should consider our early religious experience as "a portion of valid knowledge," and "cherish its emotional results in relation to objects which are either substitutes or metamorphoses of the earlier."

"And I think we must not take every great physicist—or other 'ist'—for an apostle, but be ready to suspect him of some crudity concerning relations that lie outside his special studies, if his exposition strands us on results that seem to stultify the most ardent, massive experience of mankind, and hem up the best part of our feelings in stagnation." [12]

This instinct for the understanding of all forms of thought and feeling, this quest for that which is essentially human in all varieties of belief, can of course be illustrated to any extent from the novels. "Pity and fairness," she once wrote, "embrace the utmost delicacies of the moral life," and this delicacy, together with her balanced regard for improvement and for old imperfect things, appears clearly in her treatment of contrasted types of churchmanship. Mr Gilfil's sermons (of which he kept a large heap, "rather yellow and worn at the edges") certainly belonged to the class of the old and imperfect, but when his congregation, having dozed through the sermon's "agreeable monotony," "made their way back through the miry lanes," they were "perhaps as much the better for this simple weekly tribute to what they knew of good and right, as many a more wakeful and critical congregation of the present day." [13] The same attitude appears in her treatment of Mr Irwine in *Adam Bede,* and in the contrast between him and Mr Ryde: "Mrs Poyser used to say . . . Mr Irwine was like a good meal o' victual, you were the better for him without thinking on it, and Mr Ryde was like a dose o' physic, he gripped you and worreted you, and after all he left you much the same." [14] The contrast reappears, in *Middlemarch,* in Mr Farebrother and Mr Tyke: Mr Farebrother, the man of the world who plays for money, yet who has pity and fairness, fine human tact and ripe wisdom, and knows the secret of renunciation; Mr Tyke, protégé of Bulstrode, who is doctrinal and evangelical but non-human. It was George Eliot's constant objection to evangelicalism, that in its emphasis upon the will and acts of an implacable Deity it extinguished human love and service. She extended this objection to all general ethical maxims if followed without regard to their human results:

"There is no general doctrine," she says in *Middlemarch,* "which is not capable of eating out our mortality if unchecked by the deep-seated habit of

[11] *Ibid.,* vol. iii, p. 48.
[12] *Ibid.,* pp. 245 and 253 (Dec. 10, 1874 and Jan. 30, 1875).

[13] *Scenes of Clerical Life,* pp. 94–5 (World's Classics ed.).
[14] P. 200 (World's Classics ed.).

direct fellow-feeling with individual fellow-men." [15]

Fred Vincy feels no remorse for his careless borrowings until he sees their actual effect upon the Garth family: "Indeed we are most of us brought up in the notion that the highest motive for not doing a wrong is something irrespective of the beings who would suffer the wrong." [16] "We cannot be utterly blind to the results of duty, since that cannot be duty which is not already judged to be for human good." [17] The whole analysis of Mr Bulstrode's self-justifications is meant to illustrate these principles.

On the other hand, George Eliot admires the evangelical awakener if his gospel is really constructive, if it is informed with the spirit of love: it is enough to mention Mr Tryan in *Janet's Repentance*. She laughs at him indeed, or rather at some of the effects he produces in Milby—e.g. Miss Pratt's literary effort, which was "Six Stanzas, addressed to the Rev. Edgar Tryan, printed on glazed paper with a neat border, and beginning 'Forward, young wrestler for the truth!' "—nevertheless,

"Evangelicalism had brought into palpable existence and operation in Milby society that idea of duty, that recognition of something to be lived for beyond the mere satisfaction of self, which is to the moral life what the addition of a great central ganglion is to animal life. . . . Whatever might be the weaknesses of the ladies who pruned the luxuriance of their lace and ribbons, cut out garments for the poor, distributed tracts and quoted Scripture, and defined the true Gospel, they had learned this—that there was a divine work to be done in life, a rule of goodness higher than the opinion of their neighbours; and if the notion of a heaven in reserve for themselves was a little too prominent, yet the theory of fitness for that heaven consisted in purity of heart, in Christ-like compassion, in the subduing of selfish desires. . . . The first condition of human good-ness is something to love; the second, something to reverence. And this latter precious gift was brought to Milby by Mr Tryan and evangelical-ism." [18]

Or there is her attitude to Methodism in *Adam Bede:*

"It is too possible that to some of my readers Methodism may mean nothing more than low-pitched gables up dingy streets, sleek grocers, sponging preachers, and hypocritical jargon—elements which are regarded as an exhaustive analysis of Methodism in many fashionable quarters."

But the picture she would have us form of it is

"an amphitheatre of green hills, or the deep shade of broad-leaved sycamores, where a crowd of rough men and weary-hearted women drank in a faith which was a rudimentary culture, which linked their thoughts with the past, lifted their imagina-tion above the sordid details of their own narrow lives, and suffused their souls with the sense of a pitying, loving, infinite Presence, sweet as summer to the houseless needy." [19]

Romola's attitude to Savonarola may here be recalled: it is George Eliot's own attitude to dogmatic religion. In so far as he stands for the prophetic will and insight, for the determination to bring Florence back to God, and to die if need be in the attempt, Savonarola is grand and heroic in her eyes; such absolute devotion to the highest aims and standards awes and humbles her; she forgets his superstitious beliefs and sees only the saint; she returns to Tito at his command. But when Savonarola refuses to speak the word that will save her god-father's life, all is changed:

" 'Do you, then, know so well what will further the coming of God's Kingdom, father, that you will dare to despise the plea of mercy—of jus-tice—of faithfulness to your own teaching? . . . Take care, father, lest your enemies have some reason when they say, that in your visions of what will further God's Kingdom you see only what will strengthen your own party.'

[15] *Middlemarch*, bk. vi, ch. 61 (New Cabinet ed., 1913, vol. iii, p. 133).

[16] *Ibid.*, vol. i, p. 379.

[17] Cross, *op. cit.*, vol. iii, p. 48.

[18] *Scenes*, pp. 319–20.

[19] *Adam Bede*, p. 38.

" 'And that is true!' said Savonarola, with flash-ing eyes. Romola's voice had seemed to him in that moment the voice of his enemies. 'The cause of my party *is* the cause of God's Kingdom.'

" 'I do not believe it!' said Romola, her whole frame shaken with passionate repugnance. 'God's Kingdom is something wider—else, let me stand outside it with the beings that I love.' " [20]

In her grief and rage at finding him insen-sible to human appeal, she loses all that admiration which had made her hitherto "unmindful of his aberrations, and atten-tive only to the grand curve of his orbit." It is interesting, however, that George Eliot's passion for impartiality leads her, in a comment on the foregoing dialogue, to by-pass Romola and partially rejustify Savonarola:

"It was inevitable that she should judge the Frate unfairly on a question of individual suffer-ing, at which *she* looked with the eyes of personal tenderness, and *he* with the eyes of theoretic con-viction. In that declaration of his, that the cause of his party was the cause of God's Kingdom, she heard only the ring of egoism. Perhaps such words have rarely been uttered without that meaner ring in them; yet they are the implicit formula of all energetic belief. And if such energetic belief, pursuing a grand and remote end, is often in danger of becoming a demon-worship, in which the votary lets his son and daughter pass through the fire with a readiness that hardly looks like sacrifice: tender fellow-feeling for the nearest has its danger too, and is apt to be timid and scepti-cal towards the larger aims without which life cannot rise into religion." [21]

Her typical view on the conflict between "theoretic conviction" and human tender-ness (already indicated in the extract from *Middlemarch* about "general doctrine") is to be seen in a letter to Charles Bray:

"I dislike extremely a passage [in his book, *The Philosophy of Necessity*] in which you appear to consider the disregard of individuals as a lofty condition of mind. My own experience and development deepen every day my conviction that our moral progress may be measured by the de-

[20] *Romola*, p. 508 (World's Classics).
[21] *Romola*, p. 517.

gree in which we sympathize with individual suffering and individual joy." [22]

To further this kind of "moral progress" was her most consciously held aim as a novelist, just as it was Wordsworth's aim to widen his readers' sensibility, and make them more "actively and securely virtuous." Indeed, George Eliot carries on the Words-worthian tradition in more ways than one.

"If art does not enlarge men's sympathies, it does nothing morally. I have had heart-cutting ex-perience that *opinions* are a poor cement between human souls: and the only effect I ardently long to produce by my writings is, that those who read them should be better able to *imagine* and to *feel* the pains and the joys of those who differ from themselves in everything but the broad fact of being struggling, erring, human creatures." [23]

Artistic power she defined as "an instinctive perception of the varied states of which the human mind is susceptible, with ability to give them out anew in intensified expres-sion." [24] Connected with this outlook is her deliberate renunciation of the stock themes of traditional fiction and the stage-proper-ties of "romance," in favour of that imagi-native penetration of the commonplace which she often achieves, and too often also rather embarrassingly *discusses* in the nov-els themselves. "My artistic bent," she says (and this, in a letter to Blackwood, will make no reader wince)—

"is directed not at all to the presentation of eminently irreproachable characters, but to the presentation of mixed human beings in such a way as to call forth tolerant judgment, pity and sympathy." [25]

It is when she breaks off her own narratives to justify her methods that, in spite of the interest and truth of the matter, the man-ner and tone make one writhe—as when, in *Amos Barton*, she archly rallies an im-

[22] Cross, *op. cit.*, vol. i, p. 472 (Nov. 15, 1857).
[23] *Ibid.*, vol. ii, p. 118 (July 5, 1859).
[24] *Ibid.*, vol. i, p. 174 (beginning of 1848).
[25] *Ibid.*, vol. i, p. 431 (Feb. 18, 1857).

aginary lady reader (who thinks Mr Barton uninteresting) with a "But, my dear madam"—most of your fellow-beings are "of this insignificant stamp," yet they have their sublime promptings, their sacred joys, etc., and ends:

"Depend upon it, you would gain unspeakably if you would *learn with me* [my italics] to see some of the poetry and the pathos, the tragedy and the comedy, lying in the experience of a human soul that looks out through dull grey eyes, and that speaks in a voice of quite ordinary tones." [26]

In her positive creative achievement, however, she abundantly shows the power attributed to Wordsworth by Coleridge, that of spreading the depth, height and atmosphere of the ideal world around situations, forms and incidents "of which, for the common view, custom had bedimmed all the lustre, had dried up the sparkle and the dew-drops." It was by confirming in her this conception of the novelist's aim, namely, the enlargement of sympathy by the imaginative heightening of the real, that G. H. Lewes probably rendered his most valuable service to her. "You must try and write a story"—full credit has been allowed him for that piece of wise encouragement, but what is less widely known is that Lewes had already, before their intimacy, written an essay on *The Lady Novelists* in the *Westminster* (July 1852), in which he outlined the theory that became hers—that fiction should be based on real experience, and that it should enable readers to share a profounder realization of the feelings and the plight of common humanity. He had even, in advance of his time, propounded a psycho-analytic theory of artistic creation, that it is a resolution of, and compensation

for, the artist's inward conflicts and dissatisfactions, and that feminine art is the transposition on to the aesthetic plane of the specifically feminine forms of suffering. Lewes even anticipates the illustration of the oyster's secretion, since popularized by Housman: the poem is the pearl which insulates and glorifies the pain. In a second essay, *Realism in Art* (*Westminster*, Oct. 1858), published while *Adam Bede* was in preparation, he says that "realism" should be considered as opposed, not to "idealism" but to "falsism"; the true business of art is intensification, not distortion or falsification of the real. The common appearances of daily life will furnish all we ought to ask.[27] No doubt Lewes was himself influenced here by Comte's views on the social function of the arts. . . .

The tension in George Eliot's mind between ideal and actual, action and reaction, ambition and renunciation, appears in her preoccupation with the theme of the "egotistical sublime," her recurrent treatment of efforts after sanctity, great and signal service, or self-realization—efforts which are thwarted by circumstance, "the gradual action of ordinary causes," the blight of the commonplace. We have noted the spiritual ambitiousness of her own evangelical youth—her emulation of Hannah More and St Paul, her anxiety "to be doing some little [i.e. a very great deal] toward the regeneration of this groaning, travailing creation." The content of this ambition was changed after her "conversion" (or perversion) to the Religion of Humanity, but it never left her; it remained in the form of that "terrible earnestness" we have spoken of, that sense of the peremptoriness of Duty—of duty whose claims were all the more absolute because its "divine" sanction had been destroyed. It remained, after she had found that her service must be rendered through fiction, in her haunting sense of responsibility to mankind in all that she wrote ("the high responsibilities of litera-

[26] *Scenes*, p. 48. See also the passage in *Adam Bede* (pp. 193 ff.) where she compares her methods with those of the Dutch school of painting. It contains what is possibly the most irritating remark in George Eliot's whole work: "But bless us, things may be lovable that are not altogether handsome, I hope?"

[27] For these references I am indebted to Bourl'honne, *George Eliot.*

ture that undertakes to represent life" [28]).
Of a spring trip to Italy in 1861 she writes:
"We must be for ever ashamed of ourselves
if we don't work the better for it." True,
this was written to her publisher, but it
illustrates the workings of her ever-accusing
conscience: time must not be wasted, an
account must be rendered, pleasure must
be justified by its fruits. And soon after
she adds:

"I will never write anything to which my whole
heart, mind and conscience don't consent, so that
I may feel that it was something—however small—
which wanted to be done in this world, and that
I am just the organ for that small bit of work." [29]

After her provincial salad days were over,
the thwarting, the frustration of which she
was ever conscious, came not from outward
circumstances but from her unconquerable
self-distrust: "Shall I ever write another
book as true as 'Adam Bede'? The weight
of the future presses on me. . . ."

"If it were possible that I should produce *better*
work than I have yet done! At least there is a
possibility that I may make greater efforts against
indolence and the despondency that comes from
too egoistic a dread of failure. . . . What moments of despair I passed through . . . despair
that life would ever be made precious to me by
the consciousness that I lived to some good purpose! It was that sort of despair that sucked away
the sap of half the hours which might have been
filled by energetic youthful activity; and the same
demon tries to get hold of me again whenever an
old work is dismissed and a new one is being
meditated." [30]

At those rather awful Sunday *salons* at The
Priory in later years, she always tried to
communicate, to each disciple who was
summoned to her footstool, something precious and profound—some moral souvenir
which could be taken away and treasured
for life. M. Bourl'honne thinks that George

[28] Cross, *op. cit.*, vol. ii, p. 293, to Blackwood,
March 30, 1861).

[29] *Ibid.*, p. 303.

[30] *Ibid.*, p. 306 (from Journal, June 16 and 19,
1861, written while composing *Romola*).

Eliot never attained true humility, although
she was constantly denouncing spiritual
pride and indulging in a false self-abase-
ment. But if so, she knew it herself, if we
may take the biography of Maggie Tulliver
to be in this respect (as it surely is) the
transcript of her own experience. The setting is given in that chapter on the religion
of the Dodsons ("A Variation of Protes-
tantism unknown to Bossuet") whose like
had never yet been seen in English fiction,
and which displays to the full George
Eliot's sociological insight as well as her
special gift of sympathizing where yet she
criticizes. . . . "Surely the most prosaic
form of human life": "you could not live
among such people." Let us see, she proceeds, how it affected Tom and Maggie
Tulliver—"how it has acted on young natures in many generations, that in the onward tendency of human things have *risen
above the mental level of the generation
before them, to which they have been nevertheless tied by the strongest fibres of their
hearts*" (my italics). Maggie, the predes-
tined heretic from this religion, has to endure unspeakable yearnings. "Stifled for
want of an outlet towards something beautiful, great, or noble," she stumbles upon
Thomas à Kempis, and experiences a sense
of awakening, of revelation and of conversion. "Forsake thyself, resign thyself,
and thou shalt enjoy much inward peace"—
then her melancholy, her chronic malaise,
were the results of egoism? "A strange
thrill of awe passed through Maggie as she
read, as if she had been wakened in the
night by a strain of solemn music, telling
of beings whose souls had been astir while
hers was in stupor." She sees for the first
time "the possibility of shifting the position
from which she looked at the gratification
of her own desires—of taking her stand out
of herself, and looking at her own life as
an insignificant part of a divinely-guided
whole." But what next?—

"With all the hurry of an imagination that
could never rest in the present, she sat . . . form-
ing plans of self-humiliation and entire devoted-

ness; and, in the ardour of first discovery, renunciation seemed to her the entrance into that satisfaction which she had so long been craving in vain. She had not perceived—how could she until she had lived longer?—the inmost truth of the old man's outpourings, that renunciation remains sorrow, though a sorrow borne willingly."

Inevitably, then, she dramatizes herself, sees herself as heroic in her very renunciation:

"her own life was still a drama for her, in which she demanded of herself that her part should be played with intensity. And so it came to pass that she often lost the spirit of humility by being excessive in the outward act; she often strove after too high a flight, and came down with her poor little half-fledged wings dabbled in the mud."

The same pattern appears again in Dorothea Brooke, "Theresa of the Midland flats" (the phrase I have already applied to her creator), whose sufferings likewise arose from "a certain spiritual grandeur ill-matched with opportunity." So too with Romola, with Lydgate and with Gwendolen, where thwarting circumstance assumes its most menacing shape—the incompatible marriage. The great souls in George Eliot are brought low, and come down to earth, with wings dabbled in the mud. Romola, it is true, attains a sort of ultimate deliverance, finds sanctity in service—but there is a note of fairy-tale unreality in those last chapters (just as there is, though in a different form, in the "idyllic" *Silas Marner*); the destinies of Maggie, Lydgate, Dorothea and Gwendolen are neared to her intuition. "Doing without opium" truly involves much anguish, and one can understand why George Eliot once said "it would be better if my life could be done for me, and I could look on." Bourl'honne is right, I think, when he says that "the inspiration of her work is clearly optimistic, the intention which animates it being to show the possibility of good and the power of the will; the work as it was achieved is no less clearly pessimistic, the general impression which emerges from it being the powerlessness of man against circumstances and the checkmate of the will." The keenness of her unsatisfied yearnings was tempered in her later years, but the clear-eyed endurance had strained her to excess, and the final calm seems in part to be that of exhaustion.

Barbara Hardy

Imagery in George Eliot's Last Novels

GEORGE ELIOT's last two novels, *Middlemarch* (1871–2) and *Daniel Deronda* (1876), are the most complex of her books, and the structural organization of their multiple plots seems to have brought with it, perhaps deliberately, a Shakespearean use of running images. We find single images and clusters of images which recur throughout the long narratives, the recurrence acting as a mnemonic which helps the reader to see the book as a whole, binding together past and present in anticipation and echo, and weaving the separate actions by unmistakable but oblique cross-references. Like Shakespeare's running images or like Wagner's motifs these unifying images have also the function of thematic emphasis, a function which George Eliot seems to delegate increasingly to these indirect methods rather than to the open generalization in her own voice which she uses so extensively in the earlier novels. Her own voice is still heard in the last novels, but it is sometimes silent and imagery speaks for her. This may be partly the result of her increasing interest in verse, in which case it is pleasant to find the novel benefiting from an interest which scarcely contributed to poetry, but it is more likely that it is brought about by the use of more complex narrative forms.

Her early novels are full of images, usually there to heighten an emotional appeal or to brighten a moral generalization, but the images are seldom repeated, and they are often used, especially when they are scientific or artistic, with a tone of heavy jocularity or ingenuity which carries over from her early essays in the *Westminster Review*. Where there is a sustained use of imagery it is of the naïve kind found in *Adam Bede*, where Adam thinks in terms of images drawn from the carpenter's shop, and where it is often difficult to know when he is speaking in terms of the life and laws he holds fast to and when he is making a more sophisticated attempt to look on life at large in terms of good carpentry. George Eliot is making her usual plea for our sympathy by underlining her characters' simplicity.

Yet, simple as they are, these images have one thing in common with some of those in the last books. They have a literal source. They are taken from objects which have an actual presence in the novel. Sometimes they remain real objects with some symbolic suggestion, sometimes they recur as genuine metaphor having its origin in the actual surface of life. Their literal existence seems to free these images from the tone of forced ingenuity which accompanies so many of her clever or unexpected comparisons or identifications. This solidity and ease is found in the carpentry images in *Adam Bede*, and in the river images in *The Mill on the Floss* and *Romola*, though in these last two it has the other function of giving the story a twist into fantasy. But most of these images are made directly and consciously by the characters, not by the author. It is Romola and Tito and the antique-dealer who throw out the suggestions which make Tito's armour take on a varied symbolic life, presenting fear, metamorphosis, and the life of false security, whereas one of the chief characteristics of the imagery in *Middlemarch* and *Daniel Deronda* is its gradual creation of a private ironical understanding between author and

From *Modern Language Review*, L (1955), 6–14. Reprinted by permission.

reader. The characters in these two novels are usually unaware of the significance of the images they use. They are not part of the characters' musing but part of an elaborate chain which binds character, unknowingly, with character.

This is what happens in *Middlemarch*. Here the two main themes, the theme of egoism and the theme of frustration, have their signatory images which move on from character to character. There are three important repeated images, the image of the water, the image of the dark or narrow place, and the image of the mirror.

The image of the water is repeated with variations. We meet it first in conjunction with the image of the mirror and the image of the labyrinth. Dorothea is learning to know her future husband:

Dorothea by this time had looked deep into the ungauged reservoir of Mr Casaubon's mind, seeing reflected there in vague labyrinthine extension every quality she herself brought. (Ch. III.)

On the next page Dorothea puts the image into her own words, and the shift in viewpoint brings its irony:

"He thinks with me," said Dorothea to herself, "or rather, he thinks a whole world of which my thought is but a poor twopenny mirror. And his feelings too, his whole experience—what a lake compared with my little pool." (Ch. III.)

We next meet the image in Casaubon's mind, where it is echoed with accumulated irony in his metaphor of water:

Hence he determined to abandon himself to the stream of feeling, and perhaps was surprised to find what an exceedingly shallow rill it was. As in droughty regions baptism by immersion could only be performed symbolically, so Mr Casaubon found that sprinkling was the utmost approach to a plunge which his stream would afford him. (Ch. VII.)

It recurs again, for Dorothea, after her marriage:

In this way, the early months of marriage often are times of critical tumult—whether that of a

shrimp-pool or of deeper waters—which afterwards subsides into cheerful peace. (Ch. XX.)

And a little later:

Having once embarked on your marital voyage, it is impossible not to be aware that you make no way and that the sea is not within sight—that, in fact, you are exploring an enclosed basin. (Ch. XX.)

Later images reduce even the enclosed basin; we hear of "the cloudy, damp despondency of uneasy egoism" (ch. XXI), of "the swampy ground" where his soul was hatched (ch. XXIX) and of Casaubon's "passionate longings" which "clung low and mist-like in very shady places" (ch. XLII).

Then, as far as the Casaubons are concerned, the image of water, after its significant reduction from the fountain and the sea to the bathetic basin and suggestions of swamp, is discontinued. It has done its work and the vision of frustrated enclosure is developed in other images. But we have not done with this image.

It turns up again in the parallel disillusionment of Lydgate. His lake, however, is a reality:

Rosamund's presence at that moment was perhaps no more than a spoonful brought to the lake. (Ch. XLV.)

It is echoed when his agility and power, like Dorothea's desires, are deprived of their element:

Lydgate was much worried, and conscious of new elements in his life as noxious to him as an inlet of mud to a creature that has been used to breathe and bathe and dart after its illuminated prey in the clearest of waters. (Ch. LVIII.)

On the next page the image of the mud obliquely revalues the romantic images of flowers which he has associated with Rosamund, and which her name keeps in our minds:

He could not succeed in keeping out of his mind for long together that he was every day getting deeper into that swamp, which tempts men towards it with such a pretty covering of flowers and verdure. (Ch. LVIII.)

Barbara Hardy

Here the associations with mermaids and sirens which are played on so differently by Lydgate and Farebrother are also put in their place. These images are not startlingly original in content, but in their echoing process they establish an ironical harking-back to the past and they underline the contrast and parallel which links Dorothea's story with Lydgate's. They also pick up an image which was used in the Prelude to *Middlemarch*, justifying the Wagnerian comparison. George Eliot began by saying:

Here and there a cygnet is reared uneasily among the ducklings in the brown pond, and never finds the living stream in fellowship with its own oary-footed kind.

The contrast between the great stretch of water and the shallow pond or swamp may also owe something to Bunyan's symbolic landscape. On 3 November 1843, George Eliot wrote to Sara Hennell of her "slough of despond" which she described as "the shallowest, muddiest, most unblessing stream," [1] and the slough turns up again in *The Mill on the Floss*, amongst the more conspicuous river-symbolism, and has some influence on the shifting images in *Middlemarch*.

There is another recurring image of frustration, this time one of the images caught up from the actual surface of life. This is the image of the tomb or the labyrinth. We have met Dorothea's vision of Casaubon's "labyrinthine extension" of her own qualities and the mocking "labyrinthine extent" of his work. The labyrinth begins as a compliment to unknown knowledge and turns into an image of imprisonment. Casaubon's antiquarian researches provide the source for the image, and the first doubt comes for Dorothea when he diverts the talk from the improvement in village cottages "to the extremely narrow accommodation which was to be had in the dwellings of the ancient Egyptians" (ch. III). We first meet

[1] *George Eliot's Life as Related in Her Letters and Journals*, ed. J. W. Cross (London, 1885). See also a letter of December 1848, where she spoke of being "entangled among slimy weeds."

this as an image of frustration in George Eliot's general comment on Dorothea's social imprisonment:

With such a nature, struggling in the bands of a narrow teaching, hemmed in by a social life which seemed nothing but a labyrinth of petty courses, a walled-in maze of small paths that led no whither, the outcome was sure to strike others as at once exaggeration and inconsistency. (Ch. III.)

She turns to Casaubon who walks in "vaults, taper in hand" (ch. X) as an escape from this walled-in maze, and the image returns ironically to mark her vicious circle:

But she was gradually ceasing to expect with her former delightful confidence that she should see any wide opening where she followed him. Poor Mr Casaubon himself was lost among small closets and winding stairs. . . . With his taper stuck before him he forgot the absence of windows, and in bitter manuscript remarks on other men's notions about the solar deities, he had become indifferent to the sunlight. (Ch. XX.)

Brief allusions and images gradually accumulate weight until Will's fury at Dorothea's "tomb" and "stone prison," the description of Casaubon's memory as a "dark closet," and even Tantripp's wish that the books in the library might be made into a "caticom" for Casaubon all make their contribution to the image of darkness and narrowness. The images reach a climax just before Casaubon tries to pass on his cramped researches as a legacy to Dorothea:

She longed for work which would be directly beneficent like the sunshine and the rain, and now it appeared that she was to live more and more in a virtual tomb, where there was the apparatus of a ghastly labour producing what would never see the light. Today she had stood at the door of the tomb and seen Will Ladislaw reaching into the distant world of warm activity and fellowship—turning his face towards her as he went. (Ch. XLVIII.)

And the image returns, with what must be deliberate recapitulation, when Dorothea doubts Will and thinks of him as "the spirit

80   Discussions of George Eliot

of morning visiting the dim vault where she sat" (ch. LXXX).

One of the reasons why Will's character may seem inadequate is the emotional force of this imagery. Will has to live up to the powerful images of space and light which fix him, in Dorothea's desire, as the antithesis to Casaubon. The images of space are also associated with her urge away from self. The tomb and the labyrinth are the narrowness and restriction of a woman's lot, irradiated only by feeling, but they are also the enclosed and enclosing egoism of Casaubon's world, that "mental estate mapped out a quarter of a century before . . . sensibilities thus fenced in" (ch. XXIX), the world described in images drawn from its own research. Will is "a lunette opened in the wall of her prison" (ch. XXXVIII) and when she knows that he loves her the sensation is described in terms of space and warmth:

> It was as if some hard icy pressure had melted, and her consciousness had room to expand: her past was come back to her with larger interpretation. (Ch. LXII.)

Again the images have been faintly anticipated in the Prelude, which speaks of "dim lights and tangled circumstances," and again she uses the image of herself, "groping" in "this dark, damp vault" (May 1848).[2]

When we first met the word "labyrinthine" as it was used to suggest the vast unknown possibilities of Casaubon's thought and feeling it was combined with the third prominent thematic image of *Middlemarch*, the image of the mirror. When Dorothea saw herself reflected in the waters of the reservoir, she saw a mirror reflecting herself instead of seeing through clear glass the image of the man. This use of the mirror to express the inturned vision runs through the book. Dorothea, like the cruder egoists, has to learn that each self is his own centre, and it is significant that if

she begins by looking at her own image in Casaubon she ends, in her scene of renunciation where she decides to go to Rosamund, by looking away from self through a window. The enclosure of the single point of view, the Narcissus gaze, one of George Eliot's recurring themes from *Amos Barton* onwards, finds its metaphor in the mirror.

Middlemarch is, amongst other things, a novel about distorted vision, and this image of the mirror[3] moves from character to character, making its generalization in different contexts. Dorothea's vision is distorted by illusion (as well as by shortsightedness), but there are other sources of error. George Eliot briefly surveys various views of Casaubon—Mrs Cadwallader's, Sir James Chettam's, Mr Brooke's and Celia's—and comments:

> I am not sure that the greatest man of his age, if ever that solitary superlative existed, could escape these unfavourable reflections of himself in various small mirrors; and even Milton, looking for his portrait in a spoon, must submit to have the facial angle of a bumpkin. (Ch. X.)

It is not only other people's view of Casaubon which interests her, and she looks also at his vision of the world outside himself. His impediment is egoism:

> Will not a tiny speck very close to our vision blot out the glory of the world, and leave only a margin by which we see the blot? I know no speck so troublesome as self. (Ch. XLII.)

But to return to the mirror. The fullest statement of this theme of the shifting and separate centres of vision is the elaborate image of the pier-glass, at the beginning of chapter XXVII. This turns, after some characteristic generalization, to Rosamund, but it echoes what we have already heard of Casaubon, that Dorothea came gradually to realize:

> With that distinctness which is no longer reflection but feeling—an idea wrought back to the directness of sense, like the solidity of objects—

---

[2] Cross, *op. cit.*

[3] George Eliot uses the image of the mirror ("doubtless defective") in her discussion of the novelist's vision in chapter XVII of *Adam Bede*.

Barbara Hardy

that he had an equivalent centre of self, whence the lights and shadows must always fall with a certain difference. (Ch. XXI.)

This is rather a mysterious metaphor, with self apparently conceived of as a source of light, until we find the repetition and explanation in the image of the pier-glass. Like Rosamund, Casaubon is the light reflected in the mirror:

Your pier-glass or extensive surface of polished steel made to be rubbed by a housemaid, will be minutely and multitudinously scratched in all directions; but place now against it a lighted candle as a centre of illumination, and lo! the scratches will seem to arrange themselves in a fine series of concentric circles round that little sun. It is demonstrable that the scratches are going everywhere impartially, and it is only your candle which produces the flattering illusion of a concentric arrangement, its light falling with an exclusive optical selection. These things are a parable. The scratches are events, and the candle is the egoism of any person now absent—of Miss Vincy, for example. (Ch. XXVII.)

There are many other images of distorted or inadequate vision, including the double image of telescope and microscope applied to an examination of Mrs Cadwallader's motives, and the calm and illusionless vision of Mary Garth, contemplating other people's egocentric illusion, which made their own "lies opaque while everyone else's were transparent, making themselves exceptions to everything, as if when all the world looked yellow under a lamp they alone were rosy" (ch. XXXIII). But the favourite image for vision is the reflection. There are two powerful images of Bulstrode's reflection. The first comes in his interview with his brother-in-law Vincy:

This was not the first time that Mr Bulstrode had begun by admonishing Mr Vincy, and had ended by seeing a very unsatisfactory reflection of himself in the coarse unflattering mirror which that manufacturer's mind presented to the subtler lights and shadows of his fellow-men; and perhaps his experience ought to have warned him how the scene would end. But a full-fed fountain will be generous with its waters even in the rain, when

they are worse than useless; and a fine fount of admonition is apt to be equally irrepressible. (Ch. XIII.)

Here is an interesting example of the combination of the images of water and mirror, which seems to bear a resemblance to some Shakespearian clusters. Although elsewhere each image has a similar function —both dealing with reflection, or both with contrast between fact and illusion—here the combination seems to be an accidental association.

Bulstrode's second unwanted reflection shows his futile attempt to escape from memory, reinforcing Garth's comment that we cannot escape our deeds:

Night and day, without interruption save of brief sleep which only wove retrospect and fear into a fantastic present, he felt the scenes of his earlier life coming between him and everything else, as obstinately as when we look through the window from a lighted room, the objects we turn our backs on are still before us, instead of the grass and the trees. (Ch. LXI.)

Another related image comes in the motto-heading to chapter LXXII, where Dorothea's belief in Lydgate is generalized in the lines

Full souls are double mirrors, making still
An endless vista of fair things before,
Repeating things behind.

The last appearance of the mirror image makes it an image of generous but undistorting vision—the gap between the supposed reflection in the "reservoir" and the double mirror is filled by Dorothea's progress.

Connected with this metaphor is another, that of the crystal, which appears obliquely in *Romola*. In *Middlemarch* the crystal is related rather to the group of mirror and lens images, which George Eliot uses with scientific precision and emotional urgency. This image too she uses in her letters. She writes to Sara Hennell on 18 September 1861, "I hope you have some agreeable lens through which you can look at circumstances," and just as Dorothea sees Will as the lunette in her prison, so he sees her as "the crystal that you want to see the light through" (ch. XXXVIII). When the image recurs George Eliot seems to expect the reader to be conscious of the echo, for she says "Will, we know, could not bear the thought of any flaw appearing in his crystal" (ch. XLVII).

Just as the images of flowers make an ironical link between Will's vision of Dorothea and Lydgate's vision of Rosamund, so does this image of the crystal. Lydgate's image is Will's also.

It was as if a fracture in delicate crystal had begun, and he was afraid of any movement that might make it fatal. (Ch. LXIV.)

In chapter LXXXI the image is used once more of Dorothea, with the same new suggestion of fragility: "nervous exaltation which made her frame as dangerously responsive as a bit of finest Venetian crystal."

There is another small group of images in *Middlemarch* which is plainly linked with a similar group in *Daniel Deronda*. This is a group of animal images which have a dehumanizing effect. The swamps and vaults are images which help to create character, but they have a wider thematic function as well. The animal images are used to build the portraits of those grim egoists, Rosamund and Grandcourt. Rosamund has a "torpedo contact" (ch. LXIV) and possesses "pincers" (chs. LXV and LXXVIII) and Grandcourt in *Daniel Deronda* is a masculine version of her.

Before Gwendolen meets Grandcourt she jokes about a dream in which she is "looking at the face of a magnified insect" (ch. IX). The image of her pretended dream finds its echo. When she has met him there is a new animal comparison:

Grandcourt after all was formidable—a handsome lizard of a hitherto unknown species, not of the lively, darting kind. But Gwendolen knew hardly anything about lizards, and ignorance gives one a large range of probabilities. This splendid specimen was probably gentle, suitable as a boudoir pet: what may not a lizard be, if you know nothing to the contrary? (Ch. XIII.)

Two chapters later, the lizard has become "an alligator" in the mind of Lush, who knows him rather better than Gwendolen. Later he is compared with a "sleepy-eyed animal on the watch for prey" (ch. XXXV) and, in this same chapter, with a torpedo, a crab and a boa-constrictor. Like Rosamund's, his is the egoism which grasps, encloses, and paralyses. The lizard recurs, together with the pincers (ch. XLVIII), and the last inhuman image comes just before Grandcourt's death, when the animal is "a dangerous serpent ornamentally coiled in her cabin" (ch. LIV).

This is plainly a different use of running imagery from the snowball accretions of the water and the tomb. These images depend on a much simpler kind of repetition. The villain is called animal names so often that the names transform him. This is no ironical movement from past to present or from character to character. But there is another recurring image in *Daniel Deronda* which is of the ironical stuff of the central images of *Middlemarch*. It is also an animal image, though this time it is taken from an animal which has a real existence within the novel. This is the image of the horse or the chariot drawn by horses. Katherine Mansfield noticed the passionate effect of Stephen's panting horse in *The Mill on the Floss*, and the images in *Daniel Deronda* were also anticipated by one image in *Felix Holt*, where Esther, a Gwendolen who escapes her Grandcourt, has her possible fate described by Mrs Transome, who speaks with authority:

This girl has a fine spirit—plenty of fire and pride and wit. Men like such captives, as they like horses that champ the bit and paw the ground: they feel more triumph in their mastery. (Ch. XXXIX.)

This image is repeated, with ironical flexibility, throughout *Daniel Deronda*. Its source within the novel is obvious and appropriate, for Gwendolen's imperious egoism, her ruthlessness, and her love of splendour are all shown, carefully and sepa-

Barbara Hardy

rately, in some episode concerned with riding or horses. The princess in exile, she demands a fine horse. She rides to hounds and leaves Rex to ride after her, for a fall. Her courtship by Grandcourt is almost entirely equestrian. When she has accepted him they go to the window to see the horse Criterion:

> They could see the two horses being taken slowly round the sweep, and the beautiful creatures, in their fine grooming, sent a thrill of exultation through Gwendolen. They were the symbols of command and luxury, in delightful contrast with the ugliness of poverty and humiliation at which she had lately been looking close. (Ch. XXVII.)

This is the suggestive object in literal existence, but the horse has another life in metaphor. What Gwendolen does in fact she plays with in imagination, and the modulation from the real horses to the horses in imagery seems hardly noticeable. When she is first considering marriage with Grandcourt:

> Gwendolen wished to mount the chariot and drive the plunging horses herself, with a spouse by her side who would fold his arms and give her his countenance without looking ridiculous. (Ch. XIII.)

The image recurs just before she accepts Grandcourt, when she moves in mind from one alternative to another:

> Meanwhile, the thought that he was coming to be refused was inspiriting: she had the white reins in her hands again. (Ch. XXVII.)

But when we next meet the image of the horse it is with a difference, for it is now the image in Grandcourt's fantasy:

> She had been brought to accept him in spite of everything—brought to kneel down like a horse under training for the arena, though she might have an objection to it all the while. (Ch. XXVIII.)

The clash of the separated images has its own tension, and gives life to Grandcourt's desire, which is not a crude desire for mastery, but a more sophisticated desire to master the woman who would have liked to master him, and who perhaps would have been capable of mastering another man. The coincidence of the images makes the oblique statement that two can play at metaphors. Gwendolen's image of mastering horses turns into Grandcourt's vision of her as a mastered horse.

The clash of images continues; Gwendolen is forced to change hers:

> It was as if she had consented to mount a chariot where another held the reins; and it was not in her nature to leap out in the eyes of the world. (Ch. XXIX.)

And, six pages later in the same chapter:

> The horses in the chariot she had mounted were going at full speed.

This is before her marriage. Afterwards, the images fall off, existing, like the contrast between fountain and pond, to make an ironical contrast which ends with the heroine's awakening. Grandcourt comes to observe that she answered to the rein (ch. XXXV): not only is she not holding the reins, but she is being driven, and towards the end he feels "perfectly satisfied that he held his wife with bit and bridle" (ch. LIV). This silent struggle in imagery is joined only once by another character—Deronda seems to hear Gwendolen's trust call out "as if it had been the retreating cry of a creature snatched and carried out of his reach by swift horsemen" (ch. L).

Deronda and Gwendolen share another image. This is again an experience with literal existence, the experience of wide space, which has the dual life of fact and metaphor. We meet it first in a metaphor so familiar that it is unremarkable. Klesmer is attacking Gwendolen's music:

> "It is a form of melody which expresses a puerile state of culture—a dandling, canting, see-saw kind of stuff—the passion and thought of people without any breadth of horizon. There is a sort of self-satisfied folly about every phrase of such melody: no cries of deep, mysterious passion—no conflict—no sense of the universal. It makes men

small as they listen to it. Sing now something larger. And I shall see."

"Oh, not now—by-and-by," said Gwendolen, with a sinking of heart at the sudden width of horizon. . . . (Ch. v.)

Klesmer's rebuke is the first slight felt by Gwendolen's self-satisfaction, but her fear of the widening horizon is shown as a peculiarity of her sensibility, as well as a natural consequence of being the spoilt princess:

Solitude in any wide scene impressed her with an undefined feeling of immeasurable existence aloof from her, in the midst of which she was helplessly incapable of asserting herself. The little astronomy taught her at school used sometimes to set her imagination at work in a way that made her tremble: but always when some one joined her she recovered her indifference to the vastness in which she seemed an exile. (Ch. VI.)

The relation between Deronda and Gwendolen depends very much, I believe, on our acceptance of the prominence of this theme, which establishes in imagery and in actual landscape the difference between the two, the need Gwendolen has for dependence, and the measure of her final solitude. Deronda, like Klesmer, attacks her narrowness, tries to make her understand the possibility of non-attachment, and behind the flatness of precept is his experience.

He chose a spot in the bend of the river just opposite Kew Gardens, where he had a great breadth of water before him reflecting the glory of the sky, while he himself was in shadow. He lay with his hands behind his head propped on a level with the boat's edge, so that he could see all around him, but could not be seen by any one at a few yards' distance; and for a long while he never turned his eyes from the view right in front of him. He was forgetting everything else in a half-speculative, half-involuntary identification of himself with the objects he was looking at, thinking how far it might be possible habitually to shift his centre till his own personality would be no less outside him than the landscape. (Ch. XVII.)

There is a link here with Mordecai, whose "imagination spontaneously planted him on some spot where he had a far-reaching scene; his thought went on in wide spaces" (ch. XXXVIII). This delight in wide spaces is made suggestive of the breadth of vision, the altruist's out-turned look. It is, on a larger scale, the outward gaze through the window which stamps the renunciations of Esther Lyon and Dorothea. What is triumph for them is also triumph for Gwendolen, though for her it is the cathartic shock. Just as her vision of the insect face and the dead face in the picture came to have an actual presence, like Mordecai's vision of the bridge, so her terror in wide spaces becomes an actual nightmare. This is the last image which, in its echo of what we have heard before, completes the fantasy and fixes the moral:

There was a long silence between them. The world seemed getting larger round poor Gwendolen, and she more solitary and helpless in the midst. The thought that he might come back after going to the East, sank before the bewildering vision of these wide-stretching purposes in which she felt herself reduced to a mere speck . . . she was for the first time feeling the pressure of a vast mysterious movement, for the first time being dislodged from her supremacy in her own world, and getting a sense that her horizon was but a dipping onward of an existence with which her own was revolving. (Ch. LXIX.)

I began by emphasizing the unity built by these repeated images. Perhaps I should end by emphasizing their effect of inevitability, seen nowhere so clearly as in *Daniel Deronda*. George Eliot is clearly working away from a full use of omniscient commentary, skilfully managed though this is in her novels, towards the indirect methods of hinting images. Once we find the trail the purpose is clear though the hints are often embedded in passages which we probably read more carelessly than we read the conversations or spotlighted action. *Middlemarch* and *Daniel Deronda* depend for their full effect on the kind of slow and repeated attentiveness to detail which we are more willing to give to the medium of poetry than to the medium of the prose narrative.

Quentin Anderson

George Eliot in *Middlemarch*

In *The Prelude* Wordsworth notes that while he was taken up with Godwinian rationalism he had discovered that rationalism had a special danger: it denied the existence of the passions which actually informed it. The briefest possible answer to the question, What is the greatness of George Eliot? is to say that she knew and could show that every idea is attended by a passion; that thought is a passional act. Of course it is on the showing, the accomplishment of the artist, that the emphasis must finally rest, but it seems politic to begin this account by suggesting to a somewhat unreceptive age how much she has to tell her readers. Widely read and highly respected during the last four decades of her century, George Eliot (1819–80) became schoolroom fare in ours; but the assumption that she is once more coming into the light is current, it may be the misleading consequence of the appearance of Professor Gordon Haight's monumental edition of her *Letters* and F. R. Leavis's fine chapters on her in *The Great Tradition*. There is a seeming paradox in the fact that, although admired, she is not much read, because no novelist in English has come closer to answering a question which is very important to us: How can a social world be felt and understood? It appears probable that there is some resistance in us against the terms in which George Eliot answers this question; we may well want a chance for vicarious or imagined mastery over the social order—a chance to judge and discriminate with sureness—but most of us find something remote, something truly "Victorian," in a world so fully humanized

as the world of *Middlemarch;* perhaps this is because it requires more love than we can give, more assurance than we can muster. . . .

This novel is subtitled "A Study of Provincial Life," and the climax in the national life which it partly chronicles, the period in which the Reform Bill of 1832 was moving towards adoption, was selected with the apparent intention of giving the novel the representative quality which we associate with Flaubert's *Sentimental Education* and Tolstoy's *War and Peace*. But one of the first things we must note about the novel is that this particular intention masks a more general one. Flaubert's choice of the revolution of 1848 or Tolstoy's of Napoleon's invasion of Russia as events which bring together various strands of the national experience was motivated in part by a desire to put that experience before us. George Eliot's notebook for the novel shows that she looked up such matters as the stages in the passage of the Reform Bill, the medical horizons of the 1830s, the industrial uses of manganese, and various other details. But the uses to which she puts these things are not terminal; she is not concerned as Flaubert is to lodge firmly in the reader's sensibility a mass of impressions deliberately selected to inform us of the political, industrial, and social life of the time. She is, in fact, incapable of suggesting the tone of a given period or historical moment. In the Middlemarch world, as in George Eliot generally, change is something intrusive, an irruption from without. The more general intention of which I have spoken is the attempt to render in a novel

From *From Dickens to Hardy*, ed. Boris Ford, Penguin Books, 1958. Reprinted by permission of the publisher.

her sense of the "primitive tissue" of a community.

This term is employed by Tertius Lydgate, a surgeon with excellent training, who buys a Middlemarch practice and hopes to combine medical work with research in physiology. His studies in Paris have persuaded him that a promising line of inquiry lies in the attempt to find the primal tissue which is the basis of all those adapted to special bodily functions. The master image of the book precisely parallels Lydgate's physiological inquiry: this is the image of human relationships as a web. Each of us stands at what seems to us a centre, our own consciousness, though it is in fact but one of numerous nodes or junction points. This is further illustrated in George Eliot's figure of the metal mirror bearing many scratches, which when illuminated at any given point produces the illusion of concentric circles ranged about that point. This figure enriches the suggestion of the recurrent web image and those associated with it by enforcing the fact that in dealing with a particular person we must consider: his appearance in the eyes of each of the other persons whom he encounters; the way he appears among various social groups to which he is known or which know of him; and his own complex of feelings which leads him to offer the world a version (or various versions) of himself. This does not at first seem an epoch-making kind of viewpoint for a novelist, since all novelists must somehow convey the quality of each character's self-regard and the opinions that others have of him. But George Eliot's special success in *Middlemarch* is the consequence of making the reciprocal workings of self-regard and opinion primary—in effect an extraordinary economy of means, and not simply of means, for it appears when we look closely that the matter of the book is people's opinions about one another, and that its particular method consists in contriving scenes in which the disparity between the intentions of agents and the opinions of observers is dramatically exhibited. This consistency of method accounts for our sense of the unity of a book which embraces a whole social order and four, or by another reckoning, five principal stories.

Of course these stories are intertwined by the plot as well as by our developing sense of Middlemarch as a community. The first of these stories is that of Dorothea Brooke, which was begun as an independent tale and later worked into the plan of the larger novel. Dorothea is somewhat externally characterized in a brief "Prelude." She belongs to a group of great spirits who remain unknown and unsung: "with dim lights and tangled circumstance they tried to shape their thought and deed in noble agreement; but, after all, to common eyes their struggles seemed mere inconsistency and formlessness; for these later-born Theresas were helped by no coherent social faith and order which could perform the function of knowledge for the ardently willing soul." The account concludes: "Here and there is born a Saint Theresa, foundress of nothing, whose loving heart-beats and sobs after an unattained goodness tremble off and are dispersed among hindrances, instead of centring in some long-recognizable deed." F. R. Leavis discerns a tendency on the part of George Eliot to make rather too personal investments in her heroines, and the tone of this "Prelude" bears him out. The reader ought to be assured that the Dorothea he meets in the opening scenes of the novel is not this portentous figure, but a young lady whose foible in marrying an elderly pedant has the consequences—comic, pathetic, and even, in a minor and domestic key, tragic —that we might expect it to have in life. As the novel goes forward, however, Dorothea's demand that the world afford chances for heroic achievement does begin to seem much too categorical. We must return to the question of her role in the imaginative economy of the novel at a later point.

Lydgate, the principal figure of the second intrigue, is closer to the working centre of the book than Dorothea, since his fate turns not simply on his marriage to Rosamond Vincy, but upon the sum of his actions and reactions in response to Middlemarch. His story is linked with the third in the group of four, the story of Bulstrode, the banker guilty of moral defalcations, whose self-arraignment is one of the finest episodes in the book (although the whole Bulstrode strand in the novel is less impressive than the others because his past is somewhat stagily rendered and the agents out of that past who hunt him down seem melodramatic conveniences). The fourth strand, closer in tone to the earlier Midland novels, functions in part to provide a standard by which the others may be placed and judged. It involves the Garth family, Mary, her father, Caleb, her successful suitor Fred Vincy, and the Reverend Farebrother, who also aspires to Mary. Here also belong the provincial humours of the book, which centre about old Peter Featherstone's disposition of his property.

Middlemarch is carefully (contemporary readers tend to say exhaustively) plotted. One or more of the characters in each of the four stories plays an important part in each of the other three. The Victorian reader was offered a multiplicity of occasions for sympathetic concern. One of the things about George Eliot and her readers which it is hardest for us to recapture is the artless and unashamed emotionalism of the latter over the fate of her characters, and the benign acceptance of this situation on the part of the writer. The century which wrenched Hamlet out of *Hamlet* had not the least scruple about lobbying for its favourite character while the novel was in the course of publication in parts—while it was in fact still being written. One may imagine that if the modern objection to such innocence about the fashion in which a work is made an artistic whole had been stated it would have been met with the response that the whole was really constituted by the assurance of moral conformity

—George Eliot could be trusted. Blackwood, George Eliot's publisher, wrote her in this vein while *Middlemarch* was appearing; he sets down his hopes and fears for the characters, and tells her in effect that her interposition in their lives has been both touching and morally impeccable. The novelist and her fellows were of course affected by this atmosphere: they wrote with a consciousness of the awakened and palpitant sensibilities of the readers who were speculating about what would happen in the next part; they watched the sale of each part with anxiety, and made anxious inquiry about a falling-off. Some of the occasions for sympathetic concern in this novel may be listed: How will Dorothea awake to a consciousness of the meaning of her marriage to the pedant, Casaubon? Will Fred Vincy inherit old Featherstone's money? Failing that, will he reclaim himself and marry Mary Garth, or will Farebrother cut him out? Will Rosamond's "torpedo contact" paralyse her vigorous husband, Lydgate? Can he succeed in medical practice in the face of the bigotry of Middlemarch? Can he extricate himself from his debts? How will Bulstrode be found out, and what will thereupon happen to him and his devoted wife? There is a cognate familiarity about many of the motifs of the story: the idealism of Dorothea, the earnest and rather wry Christianity of Farebrother, the weakling reclaimed in Fred Vincy, the dryness, harsh fun, and moral beauty of the plain Mary Garth. Neither plot nor traits of character taken alone are sufficiently distinctive to set this novel apart from others. I have found that youthful readers nowadays are restive when confronted by such careful plotting and such familiar traits of character; they shy away and quite miss the light which illumines all these things in their mutual relations, the voice of the wise woman. That voice is often heard speaking directly with an authority which makes use of the Victorian reader's involvement with the characters to make him look up and look about, to see how human relations are established within the world of the story—to see the whole of what the wise woman surveys.

What she surveys may be called a landscape of opinion, for it is not the natural landscape that is dominant here. In fact, there are only two fully realized natural landscapes, Lowick Manor and Stone Court, and in these cases the landscape is realized by an individual whose situation and interests make him aware of an external world at that particular moment. For the most part we may characterize the book's use of the physical world by referring to George Eliot's own sense of Warwickshire as a physical locale which has been wholly humanized, and to the Reverend Cadwallader's half-serious remark that it is a very good quality in a man to have a trout stream. This transposition of the natural into the moral and psychological is further illustrated by the novelist's use of snatches of poetry—Dorothea Brooke's hope for social betterment "haunted her like a passion"—and we may say that the affectionate sense of nature and the objects that man makes and handles which suffuses *Adam Bede* has been deliberately subdued here. Nothing comparable to the description of Hetty Sorrel in Mrs Poyser's dairy can enter into *Middlemarch,* not because it is a more "intellectual" book, but because its immediacies are not things seen but things felt and believed. It is striking that we know almost nothing of the appearance of Middlemarch itself, although our sense of the life of the town as a community is very full indeed, ranging as it does from a pot-house to the Green Dragon, the town's best inn, from horse-dealers, auctioneers, and grocers to the lawyers, physicians, merchants, clergymen, and landowners who stand at the head of the scale. Although we see little of the activities of all these people we hear their voices, each pitched to the tone of its own desire, each capable of dropping suggestively or rising assertively on grounds which George Eliot shows to

be wholly inadequate when related to the facts of the particular case. Chapter 45 is a good instance of the masterly way in which she can demonstrate the drifts and swirls of opinion through the town. In this account of various responses to Lydgate's principled refusal to dispense drugs himself, each of the voices establishes a character so fully and with such economy that it is hard to believe that Mawmsey, the grocer, and Mrs Dollop of the Tankard have not always been known to us. Yet this single chapter does much more. In it we learn that the clouds of misapprehension and selfishness gathering about Lydgate cannot possibly be dispelled, that he is more than likely to get into debt, and that his wife's awful insularity will resist his earnest and even his desperate attempts to penetrate it. George Eliot had much earlier (Chapter 15) used her author's privilege to warn the reader of all these possibilities. "For surely all must admit that a man may be puffed and belauded, envied, ridiculed, counted upon as a tool and fallen in love with, or at least selected as a future husband, and yet remain virtually unknown—known merely as a cluster of signs for his neighbours' false suppositions." The novelist, writing of *Middlemarch,* says: "I wanted to give a panoramic view of provincial life . . ."; but what she does give is something far more active, far more in accord with the image of the web—or perhaps a vast switchboard in which every signal is interpreted differently by each receiver, and each receiver is in its turn capable of propagating in response a signal of its own with equally dissonant consequences. Yet in the end, roughly but surely, the dissonances die out and a consensus of sorts emerges, for as George Eliot remarks at one point, not everyone is an originator, and there is a limit to the varieties of error people can fall into.

The characters move in a landscape of opinion, but those who concern us have an inner life; they can look within as well as without, and measure their sense of them-

Quentin Anderson

selves against the world's demands and expectations. The economy of means and materials I have referred to consists in the use of the landscape of opinion as the scene of action. It does not exclude, it rather informs and gives depth to the conventional motifs and the conventional attributes of character mentioned above. A long quotation extracted from the description of Casaubon illustrates the method:

If to Dorothea Mr Casaubon had been the mere occasion which had set alight the fine inflammable material of her youthful illusions, does it follow that he was fairly represented in the minds of those less impassioned personages who have hitherto delivered their judgements concerning him? I protest against any absolute conclusion, any prejudice derived from Mrs Cadwallader's contempt for a neighbouring clergyman's alleged greatness of soul, or Sir James Chettam's poor opinion of his rival's legs, from Mr Brooke's failure to elicit a companion's ideas, or from Celia's criticism of a middle-aged scholar's personal appearance. I am not sure that the greatest man of his age, if ever that solitary superlative existed, could escape these unfavourable reflections of himself in various small mirrors; and even Milton, looking for his portrait in a spoon, must submit to have the facial angle of a bumpkin. Moreover, if Mr Casaubon, speaking for himself, has a rather chilling rhetoric, it is not therefore certain that there is no good work or fine feeling in him. Did not an immortal physicist and interpreter of hieroglyphics write detestable verse? Has the theory of the solar system been advanced by graceful manners and conversational tact? Suppose we turn from outside estimates of a man, to wonder, with keener interest, what is the report of his own consciousness about his doings or capacity; with what hindrances he is carrying on his daily labours; what fading of hopes, or what deeper fixity of self-delusion the years are marking off within him; and with what spirit he wrestles against universal pressure, which will one day be too heavy for him, and bring his heart to its final pause. Doubtless his lot is important in his own eyes; and the chief reason that we think he asks too large a place in our consideration must be our want of room for him, since we refer him to the Divine regard with perfect confidence; nay it is even held sublime for our neighbour to expect the utmost there, however little he may have got

from us. Mr Casaubon, too, was the centre of his own world; if he was liable to think others were providentially made for him, and especially to consider them in the light of their fitness for the author of a "Key to all Mythologies," this trait is not quite alien to us, and, like the other mendicant hopes of mortals, claims some of our pity.

Certain aspects of this passage invite attention. George Eliot is here gathering up a series of notations about Casaubon which have been established in dialogue. In doing so she becomes a sharply marked present voice. We have come a long way from Fielding's interposed addresses to the reader in *Tom Jones,* a long way from Dickens and Thackeray as well—Thackeray cannot step on his stage without shaking it or dwarfing it; the effect is always of diminution, a voice which condescends to or coos about the pettiness or charm of the creatures displayed, while Dickens's effects in this kind involve facing about, leaving the characters to fend for themselves while he carries on his special pleading. George Eliot, however, speaks to the issues of her own work, and addresses the reader in terms which set her above it but never to one side. In her "I protest against any absolute conclusion . . ." we find a gentle schoolmistress's irony which places her between the book and our apprehension of it. In this instance she is saying that we are guilty, not because we are all egocentrics by definition, but because these notations about Casaubon have indeed composed our picture of him. She goes on to indicate what she is about to do with the figure: we shall end by finding him pathetic; we are to be converted—to be forced to abandon the stereotyped social gesture which leads us to "refer him [Casaubon] to the Divine regard" and refer him instead to our own failures to get the world to concede our majesty. Her own rhetoric, the somewhat heavy verbal play of "solitary superlative," the clinical remoteness and buried scientific analogy of "what deeper fixity of self-delusion the years are marking off within him," the carefully indicated central image of the mutually mirroring selves, the fact that she is playing prologue to her own action—for each of her generalities is a forecast of a part of Casaubon's fate—are all elements of that voice which frames the whole book. . . .

Each leading character has a serious delusion: Dorothea's belief that she can do good through learning; Lydgate's that the demands of science are compatible with those that Middlemarch makes of its physicians; Mr Casaubon's idea that marriage with a beautiful and passionate young girl will bring him pleasure and repose; Bulstrode's belief that he can make an inward moral restitution for the act of misappropriating his original fortune. As Farebrother (who, along with Mary Garth, sometimes functions as a surrogate for the novelist's voice) says to Lydgate (who has been preaching his medical ideals):

Your scheme is a good deal more difficult to carry out than the Pythagorean community though. You have not only got the old Adam in yourself against you, but you have got all those descendants of the original Adam who form the society around you. . . .

Joan Bennett, in her sensible little book on the novelist, emphasizes George Eliot's observation about the medium in which her characters move: "It is the habit of my imagination to strive after as full a vision of the medium in which character moves as of the character itself" (Cross, II, 10). *Middlemarch* authorizes an extension of this principle; George Eliot has created a common medium which completely immerses most of the characters. It is hard to conceive how an individual can on this scene really originate anything. Dorothea's wide charity finds no direct expression; Lydgate's scientific interest in the town's health meets blank incomprehension and effectual resistance, not only from all ranks in the medical hierarchy but from almost every element in the town. Indeed, the reader may by now feel (partly because I have played down the humour of the book)

that Middlemarch is as oppressive as that provincial town inhabited by Emma Bovary in another study of the *mœurs de province*. In Flaubert's book there are at least the passionate impulses of Emma to combat her stifling world. What is there here? . . .

George Eliot is present as the only fully realized individual in her book. This sounds like a harsh saying, but it may not be quite so harsh as it sounds. When one is reading *Middlemarch* there are many moments when one looks up and says, "How intelligent, how penetrating this woman is!" And, of course, one is speaking of George Eliot. In reading the fine chapter of analysis which has to do with Lydgate's character and the situation in which he finds himself in Middlemarch, we come upon this passage:

He was at a starting-point which makes many a man's career a fine subject for betting, if there were any gentlemen given to that amusement who could appreciate the complicated probabilities of an arduous purpose, with all the possible thwarting and furtherings of circumstance, all the niceties of inward balance, by which a man swims and makes his point or else is carried headlong. The risk would remain, even with close knowledge of Lydgate's character; for character too is a process and an unfolding.

Those who like *Middlemarch* take pleasure in the writer's judiciousness. They are far more tempted to invest themselves with her sensibility than they are to identify themselves with that of any of her characters. It is notable that analytic passages like the one just quoted predominate among those chosen for quotation from Leslie Stephen's day to our own. The description of Caleb Garth, of Rosamond Vincy's terrible self-absorption, of Dorothea's aspirations and her blindness to her sister Celia's world, of Bulstrode's casuistical inner life, of Casaubon's tortured consciousness of inadequacy—all these are analytic though all are matched by passages of dialogue in which their substance is exemplified. Certain dramatic scenes—that between Dorothea and Rosamond in particular—are also favourites, but again the most familiar passage about Rosamond seems to be that which describes her reaction to the awful, the inconceivable fact that there is another self in the world, one which Ladislaw cherishes far more than hers. These fine and satisfying analytic passages are not additions or decorations, nor do they represent a division within George Eliot, rather they exhibit her sense of process at work within the frame of actuality; it is her life *in* the novel which lies at its heart; this is what we rejoice in. Admittedly this means that no character is freed to exist as Don Quixote or Julien Sorel are enfranchised; the very firmness and clarity of George Eliot's vision, extending to the edges of her canvas, quite preclude her granting to any one of her creatures the authority of existence. Like a goddess, she suffers them to exist in so far as they may be known through sympathy and comprehension. No more life than this can emerge —any further measure would make her characters novelists. Those who are her surrogates, her delegated voices, are in a sense independent of her, but they are wholly caught up within a system of morally and aesthetically statable responses— as is Mary Garth—and correspond rather to Mary Anne Evans, who had once lived within a provincial society, than to George Eliot, the novelist.

Those who live completely within the shelter of a community never apprehend it as an entity. In a sense, the very notion of "society" came to imaginative fulfilment for the first time in nineteenth-century romanticism; the assumption of one of the roles of the romantic involved a reciprocal identification: here am I, a discriminable self, there is the world, the other to which I stand opposed. Of course such opposition was never total; the romantic was forced to call on some aspect of existence for support and sanction—on nature, on the philosophic status of the imagination, on libertarian politics, on the wider experience of the remote and exotic—whatever might give poetic actuality to the insights of the self. To George Eliot, a member of a succeeding generation, all these options were familiar, but none of them was acceptable. The experience which gave society objectivity for her was the loss of her religious faith. And the striking thing is that she did not thereupon become a rationalist, a scientific bluestocking, or a lecturer on the rights of women. Only a few months after she had informed her father that she could not in conscience accompany him to church she realized that her fresh point of view towards the meaning of religion made such gestures unnecessary and foolish. She had made a massive discovery.

This discovery was very simple, but its effects were profound. Miss Evans repossessed the world imaginatively when she came to the conclusion that the creeds, formulae, practices, and institutions in which people shrouded themselves were no less significant if one saw that they were not absolute. With a feminine directness she now accepted everything she had momentarily rejected. But human behaviour was now seen as a set of symbolic gestures expressive of individual needs and desires. The positivism of Auguste Comte undoubtedly played a role in this, but it did not teach her to interpret human actions; it is clear that this was a spontaneous gift which was hers before she began to write fiction. She was able to see the emotional concomitants of churchgoing; able to make out what Diderot calls the "professional idioms" of behaviour. Each of us is like the marine animal which borrows a shell; we borrow our shells for social purposes, but our feelers wave no less expressively for that. George Eliot found that she could translate the psychic gestures involved in our religion, our politics, our superstitions, our local traditions, and discover, as she had in herself, a common root of action and reaction. She wrote to the American novelist, Harriet Beecher Stowe, that her novel, *Oldtown Folks*, showed a comprehension of the "mixed moral influence shed on society by dogmatic systems," which was "rare even among writers." She saw, in other words, that the interplay between creeds, ideas, and desires was the novelist's business. But we must still ask what binds the novelist's world together? What sanction remains after the absoluteness of creeds and institutions has been denied?

A curious inversion in a sentence from the "Prelude" to *Middlemarch* which has been quoted above supplies an answer. In speaking of those whose career resembles Dorothea's, George Eliot remarks that the "later-born Theresas were helped by no coherent social faith and order which could perform the function of knowledge for the ardently willing soul." There is a suggestion here that if you find fulfilment through knowledge you do not need the pressure of an unquestioned social order and religious faith to sustain you. This brave assumption was written into George Eliot's work and acted out in her life. Her role as novelist involved finding and telling the truth. It was not a matter of occasional didactic interjections, but of a continuously present intelligence speaking in the declarative.

There is a famous sentence descriptive of Lydgate's character which will serve as a leading instance:

Lydgate's spots of commonness lay in the complexion of his prejudices, which in spite of noble intention and sympathy, were half of them such as are found in ordinary men of the world: that distinction of mind which belonged to his intellectual ardour, did not penetrate his feeling and judgement about furniture, or women, or the desirability of its being known (without his telling) that he was better born than other country surgeons.

The scenes in which Lydgate's character is rendered in dialogue do not have the power of this passage of commentary. The dialogue cannot render as much as George Eliot can see. I do not mean that we are not persuaded by her statement or that we feel that dialogue and statement are not in accord; it is simply the fact that she

scores most heavily as commentator that we must recognize. The very best things in George Eliot are no doubt her account of Lydgate, Rosamond, and their marriage, in *Middlemarch*, the encounters between Mrs Transome and her former lover, Matthew Jermyn, in *Felix Holt*, and the story of Gwendolen Harleth's struggle with Grandcourt in *Daniel Deronda*. In each case it is the voice of George Eliot the writer which is finally persuasive. It is absurd to say, as a good many people have, that her insight is intrusive or an aesthetic impropriety; it is her genius made manifest.

Middlemarch, the scene of this novel, is wholly dominated by the finely tempered mind which envisions it. But how is this scene framed and judged from without? What are the effectual boundaries of the landscape of opinion? The town—though it is a middling place from the point of view of one considering a group of provincial towns—lies on the marches, it is on the periphery of the great world, not simply the world of London or even Rome, but the world of science, the arts, and of history; realized human greatness does not enter it. We must inquire how the writer who herself moved in the great world acknowledged that world in *Middlemarch*.

There is a finely scaled scene in *Daniel Deronda* in which Gwendolen Harleth asks the musician, Klesmer, to help her to launch a musical career on nothing more than a feeble talent and her social pretensions. Klesmer confronts Gwendolen with the audacity and the ignorance of her claim. The scene has a wonderfully tonic effect—it is as if George Eliot had managed a dramatic confrontation of the austerities of art with the blind abundant energies of youth and beauty. Klesmer's treatment of Gwendolen is exquisitely modulated; it is at once a denunciation and a tribute to her as a woman. But she must be told that social lies and politeness have nothing to do with being an artist. In the world of art you must tell the truth; self-regard and the

Quentin Anderson

world's opinion must give way before realized mastery. There is an analogous scene in *Middlemarch*, though the standard invoked is not impersonal. Rosemary's flirtation with Ladislaw is abruptly ended when she discovers that Dorothea is all-important to him. She had found in Ladislaw a representative of the world outside Middlemarch to which she had ignorantly aspired, and Ladislaw thinks her of no account. She is momentarily awed into a generosity which brings Ladislaw and Dorothea together. Throughout the book Ladislaw speaks authoritatively about the world outside the town's awareness. It is he who tells Dorothea that Casaubon's work is useless because he has not read the German scholars; it is he who demands fidelity to a standard of artistic accomplishment; he alone has some sense of national politics.

Yet Ladislaw does not have the authority of Klesmer; he is the weakest of the major characters, not merely because he is made to behave like a dilettante, but because George Eliot's judiciousness does not extend to him; he is not understood. In fact, he is rather like a character in an ordinary novel. F. R. Leavis sees this as a consequence of the weakness of the figure of Dorothea. Since she is in part a self-indulgent fantasy of George Eliot's and not wholly disciplined by the demands of the novel, we may think of Ladislaw as an accessory required by the fantasy. Certainly the scenes they share are full of high-flown nonsense. But there is a good deal of evidence that Dorothea and Ladislaw represent something more than the unresolved longings of Mary Anne Evans. The leading characters in *Romola, Felix Holt, Middlemarch,* and *Daniel Deronda* all escape the circle of the author's judgement. It is claimed for each of them that they aspire to or escape into the great world. Dorothea is the partial exception. When confronted by her uncle, Casaubon, her sister Celia, or the Chettams, she is fully controlled, fully understood. But Romola, Felix Holt, and Deronda are all extrava-

gantly moral or extravagantly spiritual or both. And Dorothea and Ladislaw in their scenes together have the same defect.

Instead of thinking of *Middlemarch* as showing two strains, an artistically responsible element and a neurotically compelled one, we must, I believe, adopt a fresh version of the traditional assertion that George Eliot's conception of her fiction is internally divided. Leavis has pointed to the meaninglessness of the form this assertion of a split took in the criticism of Henry James and Leslie Stephen. The disjunction between an "intellectual" George Eliot and a George Eliot who has the novelist's sympathetic comprehension of human beings is, as we have seen, a clear-cut contradiction. It is the voice heard within the frame of her best fiction which has high intellectual distinction.

But there is an internal division in her conception of *Middlemarch* which corresponds to the far more serious split in *Daniel Deronda,* in which Deronda's mystical religiosity is given precedence over the fictionally superior story of Gwendolen Harleth. (The argument may also be applied to *Romola* and *Felix Holt.*) This split in the writer's conception of fiction appears to have a biographical root. The novels of George Eliot's maturity re-enact her own emancipation; the values which the Garths and Farebrother assert within the little world of Middlemarch are reasserted from the viewpoint of liberated intelligence by the voice of the narrator; her loss of faith, her translation to the metropolis, her defiance of propriety in living with Lewes, are all justified by the activity of the novelist who surveys Middlemarch. The right opinion of the Garths and Farebrother gives way before the knowledge of the novelist. But for George Eliot the re-enactment brought with it an irresistible impulse to include a character who could function as knower, an *embodied* voice.

She was unable, even in the years of her maturest art, to conceive of fiction as a truly independent form. It would seem to have been enough to bring that fine intelligence to bear on the enclosed world of Middlemarch, but she is never content with this. She must bring forward some instance of principled nonconformity, as if to feed an appetite for self-justification. We must conclude, I think, that the fairy-tale triumph of Romola over the physical and moral ills of a fever-stricken village, and the fantastic errand which takes Deronda to Jerusalem—he is, in effect, to build a culture!—are not merely tributes to a Victorian taste for moral exaltation. They are attempts on the part of the writer to give herself a recognizable moral status.

The English novel is so much the richer for George Eliot's contribution that one may be tempted into scolding her for not doing what no English novelist of the century did: for not taking possession of the great world. Her sense of community, her finely modulated articulation of passion and idea, the clarity and firmness of her characterization—these things alone justify Virginia Woolf's remark that *Middlemarch* was one of the few English novels written for grown-up people. Since the grown-up perspective includes Flaubert and Tolstoy, we are of course conscious that George Eliot did not share their power to incarnate the great world in the lesser one, to make the novel an instrument which can register the fate of a society in the perspective of history and heroic achievement. To exercise this power she would have had to take her own splendid powers for granted, and this she could not do.

Jerome Thale

George Eliot's Fable for Her Times: *Silas Marner*

. . . It seems to me that we must take a second look at the Silas story to see what it is about and what kind of story it is. In import and in over-all tone it is clearly some kind of allegory or fairy tale. Although the insistently allegorical import may keep us from thinking of it as a piece of realistic fiction, it is constructed completely within the limits of conventional realism, with careful attention to probability and to verisimilitude of detail. This shows up even in incidental reflections of the times—its treatment of the rise of industrialism, for example, is both accurate and perceptive, and its critique of utilitarianism is a good deal more subtle than the crude attack in *Hard Times*.

We can see this story about a weaver as being in what one might call a central tradition of the nineteenth century, the tradition of the crisis and conversion—an experience we are most familiar with in *Sartor Resartus* and Mill's *Autobiography*, but which can be seen in a wide variety of poems, novels, and memoirs. The materials of the crisis vary a great deal, but the pattern is more or less constant; and in describing the resolution of the crisis the author is usually expressing his own new-found stance toward reality: Carlyle, his belief in work and reverence; Mill, his Wordsworthianism.[1]

The crisis and conversion piece seems very nineteenth-centuryish because most of the crises are bound up with and expressed in terms of issues that are remote and unfamiliar. Tennyson's anxiety about geological findings, for example, or the public concern about specific questions of dogma, may seem almost incomprehensible to us. Yet it is possible to compare them to, let us say, the disillusion of so many Communists after the Hitler-Stalin pact; indeed the larger process of crisis and conversion is the same in both instances. If we understand more readily what has happened to the ex-Communist, it is partly because we feel the burden of the issues, partly because in our time we recognize, and perhaps give primacy to, the internal aspect of the experience. Seeing it in the light of psychology as well as ideology, we are inclined to take the issues as matter rather than form.

George Eliot was interested in the workings of the soul, and so she tended to see the problem in a way that is familiar to us, if new in her time, to take large issues in terms of psychology. On the surface Silas's experience of crisis and conversion is religious, and one can even take it as a kind of allegory of the intellectual movement of the age. Silas is first seen as a member of a grubby dissenting chapel. His best friend falsely accuses him of theft, the congregation expels him, and he loses his faith and becomes a miser. After fifteen years of isolation he finds Eppie and is redeemed by his love for her. At the end of the novel we see him no longer isolated from the community, but happy, friendly with his neighbors, and a regular churchgoer. Silas's route is like that of the Victorian intellectual—from earnest belief through disbelief to a new, often secular, faith. As psychologist and as student of the new theology, George Eliot saw religion as valid subjec-

[1] Jerome Buckley's *The Victorian Temper* has an interesting discussion of this general pattern in the nineteenth century.

From *The Novels of George Eliot*, New York, Columbia University Press, 1959. Reprinted by permission of the publisher.

tively rather than objectively. For her, our creeds, our notions of God, are true not as facts but as symbols, as expressions of states of mind. Faith is good and disbelief bad, not because a god exists, but because they are symptoms of a healthy and an unhealthy state of consciousness. The novel does not give statements as explicit as this, but that is surely the inference to be made from the action.

Taken in this light, Silas's blasphemy— his statement that he cannot believe in any god but a malevolent one—is important not as a theological proposition but as an indication of some change in his personality, a change resulting from his shattering and disillusioning experience. For when he has lost his trust in his fellow men and in the only institution that seemed to offer him security and give largeness and direction to life, he is impelled to reject that institution and its account of the world. What he has lost is not a creed but a sense of the world.

And a sense of the world is what he regains upon his redemption. To bring this about, George Eliot uses the ordinary device of a fairy tale—a miracle. The situation is splendidly ironic, for the miracle— Eppie's coming—is a purely natural occurrence. Momentarily at least it deceives the myopic Silas (he takes her hair for his lost gold); its effects, however, are like those of a miracle. To use Carlyle's term, it is a piece of natural supernaturalism; it is in fact a rationalist's miracle.

Since Silas is a weaver and not a Victorian intellectual, the final resolution of his crisis leaves him believing in God again and going to church on Sunday. But his new religion is really an acceptance of the prevailing local account of the world. It is a symbol of his sense of integration, of his oneness with himself, with nature, and with his fellow men—the reflex of pleasant and harmonious experience, just as his earlier disbelief is the reflex of betrayal and injustice. He has returned not to religion but to a better state of mind.

I have emphasized George Eliot's reduction of theology to psychology to make clear her distinction between the accidental matter and the true form of man's quest for some satisfactory vision of the world (a very happy adaptation of the potentialities of the novel to the biases of Victorian agnosticism, for the English novel has been, and seems inherently to be, unreceptive to the supernatural). And the psychological approach that George Eliot employed is a highly empirical one: she wanted to describe the problem on the basis of experience alone, and to find solutions outside of what she regarded as the illusions of theology or creeds. She wanted to show what belief, what stance toward reality, could be derived from experience.[2]

This, then, is what the Silas Marner plot is about—what kind of a sense of the world we can get from experience and how we come to that sense. It is, to repeat, about attitudes toward the world, states of mind, not ideologies or creeds. Silas's ultimate solution and the process that brings him to it are Wordsworthian. During his period of dryness there are hints of what will redeem him. Seeing a dropsical woman he has a flickering of feeling and offers to treat her with the herbs his mother had taught him about. The incident brings "a sense of unity between his past and present life, which might have been the beginning of his rescue from the insect-like existence into which his nature had shrunk." When

---

[2] The reduction of theology to psychology is an interesting example of the way in which ideas enter into literature. Though the idea was by no means original with George Eliot, she was, I suspect, the first major novelist to make use of it. (The popularity of *Silas Marner* as a school classic suggests that many people did not clearly realize what George Eliot was doing.) The whole matter reminds us of George Eliot's roots in the nineteenth century. The equation between theology and psychology was further developed, and in recent years we have seen it employed by writers who have reversed the process, that is, have seen the imagination in terms of theology— Greene, Mauriac, and the recent essays in *Thought* on theology and the imagination.

his water pot breaks he has enough of the pathetic remnants of piety to save the pieces and set them together in their accustomed place. The actual redemption occurs through Eppie. When he first sees the child, she reminds him of his little sister, and he is taken back to many memories—the Wordsworthian way, joining maturity with the simplicity and purity of childhood. "It stirred fibres that had never been moved in Raveloe—old quiverings of tenderness—old impressions of awe at the presentiment of some Power presiding over his life; for his imagination had not yet extricated itself from the sense of mystery in the child's sudden presence, and had formed no conjectures of ordinary natural means by which the event could have been brought about." As George Eliot has already indicated, the root of Silas's trouble is inability to feel—delight in nature, love for others, satisfaction with himself, interest in the objects of everyday life. His emotional life shrunken and channeled into love of gold, he must at forty begin—as Mill did—to learn reverence, piety for nature and for the common details of life. And Eppie is the agent of this—"As the child's mind was growing into knowledge, his mind was growing into memory."

Such is the process that redeems Silas from a meaningless existence. Its issue, as we have seen, is a restoration of love and faith. At the end of Silas's story, we feel that the world which made him happy must be good. Certainly this is a sense of the world that we should like to accept. But our own experience and observation compel us to acknowledge that the world is not that good. Like Wordsworth's poetry, the Silas story demands certain sanguine assumptions about the world and human experience which we cannot easily make.

George Eliot does not ordinarily give such a hopeful view of life; rather, she suggests that there is much suffering, much dullness to be endured. The Silas story, taken by itself, offers us immensely more hope and reassurance than any other of

her novels, but it does so less convincingly. The belief in goodness of heart, the belief that nature never did betray, are totally unexamined. It is true that there is some equity in that Silas's suffering is compensated for by his happiness with Eppie. But this happiness comes about only as the result of a chance, or as Silas sees it, a miracle. In an extra-natural account of reality it is possible to accept chance as a symbol, expressive of providence or of beneficent order in the universe. For we allow faith to supplement and sometimes supersede an experiential account of the world. It is of course just this that Silas does. He comes to accept a reassuring view of life, embodied for him in the Church of England; and in this scheme Eppie's coming is not a miracle as he first thought but part of the working of Providence (the miracle is its own evidence for its miraculousness). But the naturalistic presuppositions of the novel, the reduction of everything to the facts of experience, rule out any such providential view of human affairs. Silas is restored and believes, but can those who do not have Silas's good luck see the universe as harmonious and beneficent, see good as conquering evil and dullness? What happens to the simple-minded Silas gives him grounds for trusting, but it seems to offer a critical mind no particular grounds for trusting, believing, or loving.

This may seem to be taking unfair advantage of the novel by applying realistic criteria to an incident which is part of a fairy tale. Certainly the coincidence and the happy ending do not bother us; they are familiar enough in literature. What does bother us is that the coincidence must stand as some sort of proof or justification for Silas's view of a providential and harmonious working of the universe at the same time that the novel works in a realistic framework of strict probability in which coincidence is forbidden as a distortion of reality. Should we say, then, that the use of coincidence is an artistic defect stemming from the expression of a vain hope?

One does not like to suppose that George Eliot meant to give us a fairy tale as a serious reflection of life. We can hardly think that like Mrs. Browning or Charlotte M. Yonge she could deliberately confound or could not distinguish between wishes and the facts of experience.

The rest of George Eliot's work, with its disenchantment, is a relevant argument here. It also is evidence for the seriousness of her concern with the problem of what kind of sense of the world our experience justifies. To resolve the antinomy at which we have arrived and see in what way we must take the Silas story, we must think of it as only one half of a novel, the other half of which is the Godfrey story.

The stories are related in a parallel and complementary way. The fortunes of the two men alternate, and there is a series of pairings in character and situation. Godfrey refuses a blessing and is unhappy. Silas accepts it and is made happy. Just as Godfrey has two wives, so Silas has two treasures, and each of the two men is a father to Eppie. Godfrey is betrayed by his brother Dunstan, Silas by his friend William Dane. Godfrey is secretly guilty, Silas secretly innocent. Dunstan and the gold are buried together, for the gold is Silas's undoing and the blackmailing brother is Godfrey's. When the gold and Dunstan's body are brought to light it is for Silas's joy and Godfrey's shame. Gold passes from Silas to the Casses, Eppie from the Casses to Silas.

All these parallels and contrasts indicate the care with which the novel as a whole is worked out; more significantly, they point to the fact that the two stories involve the same theme, that Godfrey's story is Silas's transposed into a minor key. Godfrey like Silas is alienated from himself and from society. He endures a period of desolation almost as long as Silas's—fifteen years—not warped and isolated as Silas is, but incapable of happiness, uneasy over his deceit and his failure to acknowledge his daughter. Silas's exile

ends when Godfrey's begins, and the transfer of the golden-haired child is symbolic. The general pattern of the two stories is identical, but for Godfrey there is no happy ending.

The point of the thematic parallelism becomes clear when we think of the contrast in tonality between the two stories. Remembering the Silas story we think of the fire on the hearth, the golden-haired girl, the sunny days, the garden, the bashful suitor. Even in his desolation Silas is seen against a pastoral landscape. Compare the introduction of Godfrey:

It was the once hopeful Godfrey who was standing, with his hands in his side-pockets and his back to the fire, in the dark wainscoted parlour, one late November afternoon. . . . The fading grey light fell dimly on the walls decorated with guns, whips, and foxes' brushes, on coats and hats flung on the chairs, on tankards sending forth a scent of flat ale, and on a half-choked fire, with pipes propped up in the chimney-corners: signs of a domestic life destitute of any hallowing charm, with which the look of gloomy vexation on Godfrey's blond face was in sad accordance.

All through the Godfrey story the atmosphere is dull and oppressive. The story opens with Godfrey deprived of any prospect of happiness by his marriage to a dissipated barmaid, caught unable to replace his father's money which he has given to Dunstan, and threatened with exposure by both his brother and his wife. The story ends with Godfrey absenting himself from Raveloe on the wedding day of the daughter who has rejected him. In the years between there is the guilt and self-reproach over abandoning Eppie and deceiving his wife, there is Nancy and Godfrey's childlessness, and Nancy herself, narrow, barren, just dissatisfied. Even the minor figures in Godfrey's story are unhappy: the old squire is vaguely discontented, indulgent and resentful, a figure of quiet misery. It is a world greyed throughout, given up to "the vague dulness of the grey hours." No one is acutely unhappy as Silas is, but they are people who seem to sense that they are never to have much joy, that their usual happiness is the absence of pain.

Of course, the difference between the two stories is proper enough since one is a fairy tale and the other a piece done in George Eliot's usual disenchanted realism. But this only describes the difference and does not account for it, does not tell us why the two stories are brought together, what the juxtaposition of two such different views of life means.

It could, of course, mean nothing more than an artistic failure, as in *Daniel Deronda*, where the two stories are the result of two unreconciled artistic impulses. Certainly the presence of two different impulses, or visions of life, is not in itself surprising; it occurs elsewhere in George Eliot and throughout the age. Indeed it is a manifestation of one of the largest problems in the nineteenth-century novel, one with which all of the novelists wrestled and by which some were overwhelmed. They wanted somehow to acknowledge both the truth of aspiration—which like religion and poetry may be superficially false but yet is true in some more profound sense— and the truth of experience. *Pendennis* is a good example of a work that gets caught in the problem: the novel tries and wants to be honest about so much of the unlovely part of life, but at the same time it goes soft again and again, and there are spots where the reader is embarrassed and distressed by the conflict between what the book says and what, according to its own logic, it ought to say.

Perhaps this is the reason that so many Victorian novels are unacceptable to us today: they try to embody aspiration in realism. We may cherish the aspiration, but we recognize that the empirical logic of realistic fiction cuts right through it. On the other hand, realistic fiction has a converse problem. More and more as the novel found itself committed to realism it kept coming up with gloomy empirical findings. Of course the findings are not very valid

as evidence about the world (only about the state of the literary culture), for an empirical novel does not issue in generalization. It shows, in strict logic, that a certain hero or a certain group of persons is happy or unhappy.

If, like George Eliot, the realistic novelist deals not with society or with some kind of theological or philosophical assumption but only with inner experience, he can present his hero as happy or unhappy and hope that, like all literature that is probable, the work will have its own generalizing force. Thus George Eliot presents Silas and Godfrey: both of them weak in character and unskillful in battling events, both with unhappiness thrust upon them. Godfrey's story is so faithfully realistic that we have no difficulty in accepting it. And the fairy-tale treatment in the Silas story universalizes what is really individual experience, so that we feel that happiness is really possible, the world tolerable for a great many people, even though we see from Godfrey that it is miserable for some.

In *Silas Marner* the two visions, if not reconciled, are at least each given their due. And the book is seamless and free from conflict because the two visions of life are presented on two different levels so as to acknowledge that they are not directly competing accounts of reality. By putting Silas's story in the form of a fairy tale, so as to transcend that strict logic by which both stories cannot be true, George Eliot disarmed the ordinary criticism of this kind of vision (the criticism that is so devastating when applied to *Romola*): by denying its literal validity she tried to preserve its essential truth, and by presenting at the same time the story of Godfrey she gave expression to the other side of the case. Only in *Silas Marner* did she find a way to present the two visions of the world as one artistic piece. If there is no reconciliation, there is at least acknowledgment and confrontation, and for the moment we can see side by side the lamb of Mrs. Browning and the lion of Thomas Hardy.

Jerome Thale

The Darkened World: *Daniel Deronda*

... If it were not for the pun we might speak of *Daniel Deronda* as George Eliot's terrible novel. Ignoring (there is nothing else we can do with it) the Deronda half of the novel, and thinking only of the story of Gwendolen Harleth, we are struck by the darkness of the moral vision as much as by the assurance and maturity of the art. Unpleasant characters have become central in *Daniel Deronda*; Gwendolen, Grandcourt, Lush can, in one sense of the word, be described only as perverse. And their evil has the added horror of insidiousness, for it is perfectly civilized, in no way expressed through direct action. Tito Melema in *Romola* was simply a Renaissance villain, mechanically conceived. Grandcourt is not only a more credible and more oppressive presence; he cannot be described in the ordinary categories of vice, and he is beyond the bounds of sympathy, perhaps even of hate. Though Gwendolen does not go quite beyond the range of sympathy—it would be a sadistic moralist who could be neutral before so painful an account—she is dispassionately presented as morally sinister.

The moral horizon, too, is very different from that of George Eliot's earlier novels. It hardly needs to be said that the vision in both cases is wholly secular, for even Daniel's mission with the Jews is a matter of piety, feeling for race, and not of theology. And I think that the disparity in tone between the Deronda and Gwendolen stories can be related to the perplexities that faced naturalism in George Eliot's time. For secular ethic, drifting out of the orbit of Christian tradition, tended in the mid-nineteenth century towards extreme optimism, that of Comte, for example, and later on towards extreme pessimism, as in Hardy, or towards a terrifying secular confrontation of the fact of original sin, as in Céline. Daniel, the Meyricks, Mordecai, come from the flabby optimistic idealism which also produced *Romola;* Gwendolen and Grandcourt represent the other side of the process.

The most striking manifestation of the new development in *Daniel Deronda* is the figure of Henleigh Mallinger Grandcourt. The imagery used to describe him is insistent. He is a "lizard," an "alligator," a "boa constrictor" (how apt to describe the slow and powerful movement of his cruelty as it crushes Gwendolen). His perversity —and perhaps it is necessary to say that it is a moral perversity, a perversity of the will rather than perversity in the Krafft-Ebing sense—is large, intense, and disturbing. With the exception of Tito, George Eliot's villains—such as Godfrey Cass, Arthur Donnithorne, and even the evangelical hypocrite Bulstrode—offer some lodgment for sympathy. They are seen as people with an ordinary moral sense who want to do good even when they are too weak to resist temptation or too far caught not to do further evil. They do not mean to do evil, or prefer it. Grandcourt is very completely realized, and he does not mean well; nor is there, as with Casaubon, who is also cruel to his wife, even an oblique claim upon our sympathy.

There is a kind of atmosphere of cruelty —and even something beyond simple cruelty—about Grandcourt, and we see it

From *The Novels of George Eliot*, New York, Columbia University Press, 1959. Reprinted by permission of the publisher.

very specially in his relationship to Gwendolen. But although Grandcourt as husband is a large presence in the novel, sexuality is with him one aspect of a more general impulse to assert and dominate, as we can see in his courtship. When Grandcourt makes his offer, Gwendolen is silent. "The evident hesitation of this destitute girl to take his splendid offer stung him into a keenness of interest such as he had not known for years. None the less because he attributed her hesitation entirely to her knowledge about Mrs Glasher." Grandcourt's reaction to Gwendolen's acceptance of him is described in a passage which is surely remarkable.

She had been brought to accept him in spite of everything—brought to kneel down like a horse under training for the arena, though she might have an objection to it all the while. On the whole, Grandcourt got more pleasure out of this notion than he could have done out of winning a girl of whom he was sure that she had a strong inclination for him personally. . . . In any case she would have to submit; and he enjoyed thinking of her as his future wife, whose pride and spirit were suited to command every one but himself. . . . He meant to be master of a woman who would have liked to master him, and who perhaps would have been capable of mastering another man.

In everything Grandcourt seeks power. Not power as the ordinary ambitious man conceives it, but power conceived abstractly and free of the coarseness of personal aims. That is, power considered in relation to his will rather than to the objects or persons involved. For the sheer sake of asserting his will, and even when it is not to his interest, he enjoys doing the opposite of what people expect him to do. He will not take notice of what interests everyone else, finding that " 'It's a bore.' " And he has special pleasure in not speaking, considering most persons and subjects beneath his notice; even his courtesy is of that odious kind whose chief function is to indicate contempt.

Gwendolen, though in a less striking way, shows the same new and sinister quality. The imagery of the Gwendolen story suggests in a subtle and muted fashion the dark side of George Eliot's vision. Our first sight of Gwendolen is at the gaming table of a continental spa. She is described as a "problematic sylph" and a "Nereid." And there is a rich cluster of similar images in the comments of the onlookers: " 'She has got herself up as a sort of serpent now, all green and silver, and winds her neck about a little more than usual. . . . A man might risk hanging for her—I mean, a fool might,' " he continues playfully. " 'Woman was tempted by a serpent: why not man?' " " 'It is a sort of Lamia beauty she has.' "

The imagery here announces Gwendolen with the directness characteristic of the art of *Daniel Deronda*. Lamia, the serpent, and the other metaphors suggest—what is confirmed later—Gwendolen as attractive, feminine, and at the same time man-devouring and, in a way, sexually morbid. "With all her imaginative delight in being adored, there was a certain fierceness of maidenhood in her. "Rex Gascoigne, her first suitor, thinks of her as "instinct with all feeling, and not only readier to respond to a worshipful love, but able to love better than other girls." But as he soon finds out, the sylph becomes something else when she is made love to. She is "passionately averse" and objects "with a sort of physical repulsion, to being directly made love to." She dislikes being touched and will have no one near her but her mother. And we see the same thing in her relation to Grandcourt; she tolerates him as a lover because she does not fear that he is going to kiss her.

When she discovers that Grandcourt has kept a mistress for nine years, her revulsion is intensified. " 'I don't care if I never marry any one. There is nothing worth caring for. I believe all men are bad, and I hate them.' " And she suddenly accepts her cousins' offer of a trip to Germany. Her reaction is not a conventional disillusionment about the character of her suitor; rather it springs from her "fierce maidenhood," from the idea of Grandcourt as sexually menacing, something more than the well-bred lover who gives only restrained compliments and silence.

For Gwendolen, as for Grandcourt, there is a parallelism between sexuality and will; or, to put it more exactly, sex is with both of them a metonymy for will. Gwendolen's "fierce maidenhood" comes from her feeling that lovemaking is not so much an overture to the person as a kind of aggression against the will, which offers something that the will cannot handle. She seeks a kind of virginity of the will, in which the will is as inviolable as the body. Her fear of love is the most striking manifestation of such a feeling about the will (yet, in her portionless situation, Gwendolen must more than most come to terms with love and marriage). But her fear of death (she becomes faint when she sees a picture of a corpse), her fear of being alone, and of course her powerful desire for independence are also a recoil from things which the will cannot handle, which offer a challenge to its sufficiency. Though Gwendolen does not see the connection between fear of sexuality and her general desire for dominance, the two are closely related, and we feel at last that will is at the bottom of Gwendolen's difficulties.

Gwendolen's perversity of will is less extreme than Grandcourt's, but it is essentially the same in its movement and structure. Indeed Grandcourt's conquest of Gwendolen is made more poignant because the two are so similar. Gwendolen anticipates the delicious pleasure of refusing Grandcourt, and, even to the last, thinks that she will do so. Her triumph is to be heightened by the fact that, as the world and Grandcourt see it, the match is an excellent one and that she does have every reason to accept. And more generally, both her nature and her position lead her to assert her will through a kind of proud independence. Hence her humiliation when

Deronda returns the necklace, hence her abhorrence of the idea of being a governess.

Her will is so intense that obstacles, in the beginning at least, only serve to strengthen it. When Klesmer tells her that she cannot succeed as an actress, she redoubles her effort of will: " 'It is useless to cry and waste our strength over what can't be altered. You will live at Sawyer's Cottage, and I am going to the bishop's daughters. . . . We must not give way. I dread giving way.' " Her final acceptance of Grandcourt shows the same kind of resistance before opposition; first she hopes to dominate and then resolves that no one shall know her humiliation, that she will not give way to disappointment or resentment.

The book opens with the image of Gwendolen at the gaming table, and it was from such a scene that the germ of the novel came to George Eliot. The scene prophesies Gwendolen's course—the transactions with Grandcourt where she at first wins, then loses, and then resolves to lose strikingly. It also describes the quality of will which is to bring these things about. Gambling points to the intense and self-destructive powers of pure will asserting itself without reference to circumstance, and Gwendolen's response to gambling is emblematic of her attitudes throughout the novel. When she starts to lose at roulette, her companion urges her to leave.

For reply Gwendolen put ten louis on the same spot: she was in that mood of defiance in which the mind loses sight of any end beyond the satisfaction of enraged resistance; and with the puerile stupidity of a dominant impulse includes luck among its objects of defiance. Since she was not winning strikingly, the next best thing was to lose strikingly.

From another point of view Gwendolen's progress is concerned not with the will but with the world outside her; it is an initiation into evil. But the very force and quality of her will work to keep her ignorant, innocent. For her will constructs

Jerome Thale

an account of reality in which obstacles to the will do not seriously exist. In fact the most serious obstacle to the will—or to Gwendolen's will—is the evil actions of others. Her scheme of reality—the game that she plays—demands that others do not do evil, that they act according to the rules, if the opportunism which is her assertion of her will is to succeed. Evil is something that pure will cannot deal with. Gwendolen discovers that evil exists in the real world (as it does not in her will) and that she is compelled to act in the face of it. And since the real world does not give way, is harder and tougher than the will, Gwendolen is gradually coerced to an acknowledgment of the insufficiency of the will.

At the beginning of the novel, Gwendolen is knowledgeable enough; she does not have, or manages not to display, the inexperience of the girl of twenty. If she exaggerates her own knowledge and competence, she is quick enough to keep from being caught. But her notions of evil in the world and others are imperfect—at once sophisticated and girlish. Least of all can she see evil in herself, or even see herself in the wrong. As she goes through much of the world, she finds that it scarcely squares with a clever and high-spirited young girl's idea of it. But her obduracy and resilience are so great that her real knowledge of evil comes only through her closest personal relationships. Though Gwendolen is shrewd about people, her egoism blinds and cramps her imagination; thus she can manipulate others but she cannot understand their natures or predict what they will do. Mrs. Glasher opens some new possibilities to Gwendolen. But her principal discovery comes through Grandcourt. For his perversity—though the novel does not force the point upon us—is an extension and exaggeration of her own tendencies. She has thrust upon her a series of experiences which show her the terrible cruelty beneath Grandcourt's correctness and at last suggest to her—

what she could scarcely have guessed—the possibility of her own corruption.

Sex is a kind of focus for Gwendolen's discovery of evil. The fierce maiden, the Diana, finds not an Endymion but Grandcourt. And, as we have seen, sex is for Gwendolen ugly and fearful in itself, and it is as much a violation of the purity of the will as of the body. At one point Gwendolen sees before her two choices: a career in the theater or marriage with Grandcourt; both options are sexually fearful, as Klesmer and Mrs. Glasher make clear to Gwendolen. But one of the two she must choose. (Mirah is in a similar predicament, but her situation is as conventional and melodramatic as Gwendolen's is real and frightening.)

Gwendolen's confrontation with sexuality is simultaneous with and contributes to a more central process, her discovery of the inadequacy of pure assertion of the will. The movement of the novel is a contrapuntal one. It proceeds on the one hand through a series of assertions of Gwendolen's will: gambling, the coquettish acquaintance with Grandcourt, the flight to the continent, the rejection of the position as governess, the proud acceptance of Grandcourt, and finally the determination to make the best of the marriage and not to resist openly. On the other hand it moves as a series of checks to her will: Daniel's disapprobation of her gambling and her discovery that she cannot ignore his disapproval; the humiliating return of the necklace; the loss of the family fortune. These reverses, except for the first, are more or less external and can be dealt with by a stiffening of the will, but they are followed by a series of catastrophes which the will cannot successfully counter. Gwendolen is shocked by Klesmer's discouraging verdict about her talent and by his account of the hard work and time involved in a theatrical career. Then there is Mrs. Glasher's revelation—something Gwendolen's will cannot deal with adequately because she has never recognized such situations as possible in her experience. And the last check—the one that renders Gwendolen's will incapable of asserting itself—is the marriage to Grandcourt. Gwendolen's disillusion and frustration are the greater because she has not expected much and thinks she has no illusions, anticipating that if she cannot dominate Grandcourt, she will at least have greater freedom and will put up with him in a dignified way. But what Gwendolen gets is beyond her previous power of imagining. Even acceptance is impossible under Grandcourt's pressure to master, and Gwendolen's will is completely checkmated.

It is checkmated because more and more it has become involved in concrete circumstances. In a void the will constructs or reconstructs the outer world and allows neither evil nor obstacles. But in the real world both exist, choice is limited, exclusive. At the beginning, with no ties and enough money, Gwendolen can have the illusion of the sufficiency of the will, but as she moves from pure assertion of will to action in the face of people and events, the will is stopped and turns back upon itself in paralysis and self-accusation.

Gwendolen's will resists the checks at first, but as the reverses become so large that they cannot be resisted they begin to render her more receptive to the idea of the limitation of will and the intractability of circumstances. Like Raskolnikov, she undergoes a process the issue of which is remorse and acknowledgment of guilt. But the process is not so much a coercion to remorse as it is a development of the moral sense to a point where it can admit good and evil, guilt and innocence; only when the dry ground of the ego has been broken is moral judgment possible. As James says, "Her conscience doesn't make the tragedy; that is an old story and, I think, a secondary form of suffering. It is the tragedy that makes her conscience, which then reacts upon it; and I can think of nothing more powerful than the way in which the growth of her conscience is traced, nothing more touching than the picture of its helpless maturity."

Earlier in her career George Eliot had asserted that "the highest 'calling and election' is to *do without opium* and live through all our pain with conscious, clear-eyed endurance," and there is no reason to think that she abandoned the idea. But only in *Deronda* has the fullness of her disenchantment worked itself out in the fullness of her art. Gwendolen's conversion shows us how much deeper and darker a meaning the sentence has in *Daniel Deronda*.

By George Eliot's time the notion that human beings act for self-interested motives and that they are to be understood in terms of naturally explicable causes had been thoroughly domesticated. But a person more sensitive and imaginative than the nineteenth-century economists or political theorists may find in that idea something terrible and perverse. He may discover that the world contains not only the open and somewhat commonplace selfishness of Sir Hugo Mallinger, but the subtle, involuted, and purely destructive egotism of Henleigh Mallinger Grandcourt. He may see not only moral natures, but moral processes, differently and more starkly.

Gwendolen's suffering does not ennoble, it makes the sufferer more miserable, increases self-hatred, and like a fever must get worse before it can get better. And with what a terrible and uncompromising naturalism the process is imagined. From the moment when Deronda looks at her, Gwendolen feels self-reproach, and this is the agent of her regeneration. Deronda is not, as has often been said, her confessor; he is a lay analyst, and a poor one; he conducts her through the dark night of the super-ego, urging her to self-reproach, to fear of self and of consequences. He feels her regeneration is nearly complete when she accuses herself of murdering Grandcourt, seeing in this a "sacred aversion to her worst self."